I
Am
Here

Opening the windows of life and beauty

I
Am
Here

Opening the windows of life and beauty

Georgi

BOOKS

Winchester, UK
Washington, USA

First published by O-Books, 2014
O-Books is an imprint of John Hunt Publishing Ltd., Laurel House, Station Approach,
Alresford, Hants, SO24 9JH, UK
office1@jhpbooks.net
www.johnhuntpublishing.com

For distributor details and how to order please visit the 'Ordering' section on our website.

ISBN: 978 1 78279 426 4

A CIP catalogue record for this book is available from the British Library.

Design: Lee Nash
Cover Art copyright: Willem Janssen, theartofchi.com

Printed and bound by CPI Group (UK) Ltd, Croydon, CR0 4YY

We operate a distinctive and ethical publishing philosophy in all
areas of our business, from our global network of authors to
production and worldwide distribution.

CONTENTS

This book is dedicated to Bart ten Berge, my muse, lover, friend, protector and an adorable gift to humanity. This is an offering for the one who gives so much, and for whom every creation is a celebration of love. I am here for you.

Now is the time to open the inner windows of perception
and to allow the ecstasy, bliss and passion of creation.

I AM HERE

I

I Am Here

I

Summary and Introduction

The powerful wakefulness of consciousness allows, generates, penetrates and releases experience. This is the blissful light of awakening through which we can witness all things, even consciousness itself.

Consciousness can divide, multiply, focus and create. It is a protector, a teacher, a gatekeeper and that which surrenders all that magnificent power and freedom to aspects greater than itself.

With our consciousness, we organize linear time – from the 24-hour clock, through to the construction of sequences of cause and effect, thus composing our stories, processes and understanding our direction.

Within individual consciousness is the deep imprint of the highly special manifestation of the individual, unique in the universe, moment by moment.

As consciousness moves into deeper embodiment in physical form, it emanates the experience of bliss.

At the eye of consciousness is the witness: that which sees and records all manifestation as it emerges into the field of knowledge.

Through our consciousness, we can enter the stillness of silence and become blessed with the universal presence of peace.

AM

The inclusive plane of awareness softens, accepts, blesses and blends with the miracle of phenomenon, allowing all polarity at the junction of heaven and earth and of one soul with others.

Awareness opens emotional memory, or sentient time. This is

the time needed for feelings associated with human life to be processed, integrated and released back to source.

It is the carrier of unconditional love and can open ecstasy. It blows over and through space and form. It flows with rivers of life across the rifts inherent in creation. It is the harbinger of unity, a field of existential integration into embodiment, the vehicle of empathy and the destiny of compassion.

At the source of pure awareness is the observer – that which contains all phenomena unconditionally, from within and behind each particle of experience.

Through our awareness, we can open the inheritance of our qualities or talents, and behind that, reside in the stillness of being, present in the sanctity of universal love.

HERE

Containing it all, perception through emptiness is the source of inherent liberation from experience. It is present in the space between and within each atom and particle. It is the infinite backdrop of physical form.

Moving with a skill to disillusion, it brings a clear sight that perceives the universal backdrop to every miracle of creation and destruction.

Within the dimension of emptiness, all transient form is empowered with the fullest right to exist. Perceiving through and beyond all things, emptiness opens a passion of service to life itself.

Within perception through emptiness is an allowance of physical time – the life cycles of birth and death, growth and aging, inherent to the physical plane.

Perception through emptiness is existential, as the transience of all phenomena affirms the indivisibility of existence itself, before, within and behind all manifestation.

Through emptiness, we can access the stillness of intransience and find infinite strength in the universal fact of unity.

Perception: The 3 Windows
Turn within. Keep moving until you find a space where you can manifest peace, love, or unity. Be that. Live it.

Summary

You can use the following summary for clarification and as a reference and support for understanding the words chosen to define that which will ultimately always defy definition. The glossary at the end of the book will also bring clarity to the specific use of language used in this book.

Consciousness

Linguistic presence: I
Trace: Unique individuality
Active seed: The Witness
Energetic point of initiation: Centre of the head
Spiritual outcome of development: Awakening
Aspect of Process: Cognition
Process Container: The Unknowable
Human gift: Free will
Soul connection: PEACE
Active: Penetration
Receptive: Absorbing
Still: Silence
Polarity: Male
Vibration: White/Silver
Element: Light
Sense: Sight
Human experience: Bliss
Heart level: Wisdom
Examples of attributes:
Peacefulness, authority, charisma, protection, power, respect, creativity, responsiveness, mediation.

Examples of afflictions:
Abuse, war, psychopathy, domination, repression, rigidity, destruction, jealousy, control, terror, fear.

Awareness

Linguistic presence: AM
Trace: Talents, qualities
Active seed: The Observer
Energetic point of initiation: Centre of the heart chakra or chest, inside the spine
Spiritual outcome of development: Enlightenment
Active: Healing
Receptive: Acceptance
Still: Pure Being
Aspect of Process: Sentience
Process Container: The Unrevealed
Human gift: Integration, healing
Soul connection: LOVE
Polarity: Male-Female, heaven-earth
Vibration: Yellow/Gold
Element: Water
Sense: Sound, vibration
Human experience: Ecstasy
Heart level: Compassion
Examples of attributes:
Happiness, kindness, sensitivity, empathy, softness, inclusivity, acceptance, expansion.
Examples of afflictions:
Depression, grief, abandonment, betrayal, loneliness, rejection, helplessness, despair.

Emptiness

Linguistic presence: HERE
Trace: Strength
Active seed: Will, intention
Energetic point of initiation: Centre of the tailbone (coccyx)
Spiritual outcome of development: Liberation
Active: Realization
Receptive: Release
Still: Eternity
Aspect of Process: Existence
Process Container: The Imperceptible
Human gift: Perspectives
Soul connection: UNITY
Vibration: Red/Copper
Polarity: Female
Element: Matter
Sense: Touch
Human experience: Passion
Heart level: Empathy
Examples of attributes: Freedom, intimacy, clarity, integrity, authenticity, purity, hope, allowance.
Examples of afflictions: Negativity, cynicism, senselessness, bitterness, mistrust, narcissism, addiction, possessiveness, obsessivity.

Introduction

"Start with the indisputable: I am here. Stay there."

This book is inspired by a process and exploration that has led to the increasing experience that these three aspects: consciousness, awareness and emptiness are three relatively divisible means of perception. Each aspect draws in and depends on the other two.

7

I (consciousness). AM (awareness). HERE (emptiness).

Or, equally of value and more directly expressing the mystical movement from the basis of the planet back to the universal source of being: HERE (Emptiness), AM (Awareness), I (Consciousness).

Or – a movement quite natural to the human being ending with a greeting of the heart: Here (Emptiness), I (Consciousness), AM (Awareness).

The all-perceiving consciousness moves through softness. The totally open awareness moves through stillness. All pervasive existence moves through emptiness. At a certain stage, softness, stillness and emptiness can come together as one harmonious atmosphere for human living.

Naturally, we use all three aspects in a synergy of perception moment by moment. Yet each aspect can be separately developed and mastered.

Some will move with a highly developed consciousness, to which awareness and emptiness take a supportive role. Others have strengthened the level of awareness, so that their consciousness moves naturally in a blend with perception through awareness. Still others move deeply through perception through emptiness – consciousness and awareness emerge and attune freely within this backdrop as relatively loose phenomena.

In the development and mastery of these three powers of perception, the way is opened to a far greater expansion, empow-erment and realism. Inner growth becomes more serious than ever before... and far less.

Mastery of the three portals of perception brings with it an increasing ability to attune how we manifest ourselves in the world. It widens our freedom in areas from healing touch, to sexuality, through to the capacity to connect to others through communication. Most importantly, it increases our ability to step behind all three channels and simply witness life as it unfolds.

Yet this is a process that can lead to the unveiling of the

deepest experiential layers of our present existence – layers of experience so habitually there in our field of perception that we have begun to take them as fixed and permanent aspects of who we are.

It is a process that can refine and develop our healing abilities and interpersonal relations. Yet it is a process that will bring with it confrontations with the very layers of suffering that have limited us until now. It will show us where we are not yet free, and where we are not yet able to accept the unity of life.

It will test the mind, body and spirit, and then it will liberate all three. There can be miracles of healing, transformation and bliss, and there can be an agonizing Via Dolorosa of rejection, a crucifixion of being, leading to a resurrection in eternity. Each authentic process heals its stigmata.

Even our worst nightmares are transient dreams like thunder clouds obscuring the sky. Through experiencing this, we can find ourselves purified with a new kind of knowledge – the knowledge which is more closely found in the biblical sentence: "and Adam *knew* Eve."

And in this we will know in our minds, in our hearts, in our blood and in our guts that we are not what we know. We are the one knowing.

Each individual who embraces such a process, arising out of the lifetime question "Who am I?" would seem to be of service to the evolution of the whole. This is because ultimately there is no such thing as 'private' liberation, 'private' suffering or 'private' happiness.

We are not truly private within our transient, fragile bodies. We are not private within our relationships. We are not private as families, or as nations. We are not even private as a species. Even planet earth, lonely as it might seem, does not exist privately or in isolation. It is part of the universal whole, on which it is utterly dependant.

The sense of privacy is a useful illusion to negotiate our way through layers of fear and suffering. It is a transient protection, like a screen between ourselves and others; or a shield between our ideas of selfhood and the one we truly are.

Right now, in this moment, we are in it together. We are one.

If we will not engage in this deep stage of inner growth on behalf of our own being, we might well do it for others, especially those to whom we have dedicated our lives, such as our children.

A journey is beginning in which our fear of the unknown is indicating a need to allow the infinitely known.

All of us are precious to creation: every shiver of every experience – be it good, bad or ugly – is contributing to the whole.

Through deepening and expanding our mastery and connection with the means of perception, we open new possibilities in relationships; we become less limited by our past and less defined by the future. Everything is possible.

Through understanding how we experience the world – and interact with it – we liberate a wider promise for self-development and shared evolution.

In mastering the tools of perception, you will find a greater liberation, one that can allow both an individual and a greater unity to coexist in the drama of creation.

We become of service to life itself.

2

Come to Life

"Turn within. Give space to the inner world. It is worthwhile to go there."

There is one experience or phenomena at the essence of all that you know and are, and behind all that you have ever known or experienced or will ever know or experience.

It is behind and unconditional to every feeling, pain, process, understanding and endeavour. It will never leave you. This is the living fact of your existence: the life which is who you are – existing right now, in this moment.

This simple and clear existence is who you are and is inherent to every detail of form, experience and perception. It is the powerful, unconditional, liberated manifestation of existence itself. You.

Such a statement can seem blindingly obvious, but don't be blinded. The mind has a tendency to desire absolute reign over the greater power of your life. Release the mind and tap into a living sense of existence. It is not a dead-end street, but the beginning of the journey you came here for.

Our generation has seen the birth of a new age of spiritual searchers and teachers. Beyond the framework of conventional religion, these brave individuals and groups are uncovering and rephrasing methods of inner inquiry through experience to awaken the promise of 'being'; to harness the power of the mysterious; and to enter processes of personal and collective empowerment, from the inside out.

Their collective message is extremely simple: "Turn within. Give space to the inner world. It is worthwhile to go there." For all the cynicism, frustration and unresolved issues, I have yet to meet an awakened friend who would choose to return to former ignorance (even if they could). With hindsight, ignorance is apparently *not* bliss. This in itself points to the value of inner growth and in developing our ability to experience life through our nakedness.

Now is a good time to get to the bottom of the riddle of why it is so hard to stay connected to our own existence. Why, between moments of awakening, do we find ourselves 'gone' as if we had not been all there, as if we had been practically sleep-walking? Why do we time and again get pulled out of our own presence and sense of natural vitality, and into entanglements of emotions and thoughts?

The more alive we are able to become, the more deep is our sense of fulfilment in our purpose as human beings. It is really worthwhile to take a step inside, into the living miracle of who we are, into the area behind perception in which we can unblock the subtle barriers to our own manifestation in physical form. Through moving into an exploration of perception, this work is possible.

This book is born of a passion to meet you in a shared journey through the opening and widening of our windows of perception. Perception, as used here, is the means through which we, as existence, experience the world, both outside and inside ourselves.

Imagine you are a castle. On the top floor, there is a turret with one small arched window. You have been told that this is the only window through which you can view the world. The room is comfortable but dull. The view is to the North only. You sense there are other rooms, other floors, and other views around this castle in which you reside. Perhaps they are dusty and abandoned, but they are part of your potential. Perhaps you even suspect that on the ground floor there is a door through which you could step out and explore the whole mysterious land. These windows are the portals of perception.

The beauty is that when you realize that you are bigger than one room and one window, that one window becomes relative and is no longer absolute. In this, just the relativity empowers the life which you are within the castle. Your existence itself begins to expand with possibility.

In moving into a refinement, permission and exploration of the means of perception, you will be inviting your essential existence to incarnate in form. Manifestation in human form is a precious process of bliss and ecstasy which arises when we move the passion of development.

Between this pure, individual and absolute existence, and the present experience of being in a body with all its physical, psychological, emotional and temporal layers, is your perception. This not a static thing, it is responsive to invitation, to refinement and to development.

Through mastering the means of perception, the promise of who you are in physical form is opened with an increasing opportunity for fulfilment. Through understanding, experiencing and allowing the opening of the windows of perception, you will be able to increasingly come to life as part of the awakened and responsible human community, in deepening affinity with a shared direction and purpose.

Perception is not complicated. It is a matter of softening our habitual beliefs and allowing experience. Just by allowing a feeling to exist in its totality, and through feeling the feeling with a softness and curiosity, observing its evolution, we are opening a window of perception which is other than the habitual practice of perception through the mental focus of consciousness.

In this, the mind can begin to follow experience which is a significant shift from the mind dictating the feelings we are 'allowed' to have. This is a step towards authenticity opened by allowing the window of perception of awareness or sentience. To some degree, you are doing this all the time, without knowing.

Many of us can easily use meditation to transcend the human

factor, or seek enlightenment in order to subtly liberate ourselves from human responsibility. This can only ever be a short trip – because we *are* here, and we *are* human. The human opportunity can be postponed in the hope that it will not reoccur through reincarnation, but it cannot be cancelled out.

The invitation here is to move to a degree of mastery of human living.

3

Are You 'There'?

"In the deepest pain or grief, we can be surprised by joy."

Have you ever heard the expression "He is not all there"? or found yourself alienated among crowds or co-workers feeling there is a pervasive sleep, as if you suddenly find yourself isolated in a surreal awareness of existence?

Perhaps you have noticed the paradox that precisely at times of physical death of a loved one, or a stranger, the sense of being alive becomes potent?

Surely, there are times and conditions in which we feel more alive, which live in stark contrast to the impact on our memory among long periods of half-living, as if we were not there, as if we were moving through the world in a kind of dream, hardly open to experience.

The shock of rapid change has the power to open a window to an inner space of stillness. As such, at a time of violence or trauma, we can meet an unexpected peace; or in the deepest pain or grief, we can be surprised by joy.

The very relativity of times when we are more asleep on automatic pilot and times that we feel fully alive suggest the promise of self-development. This is the promise of life – your existence – in the full beauty of fearless manifestation.

Your existence is not a static 'thing' or a concept. It is life itself – who you are – flowing from a seemingly infinite source. There is so much potential in this life that we can only contain it by degrees within our nervous system and physical form.

To begin making space for existence is to begin to fulfil the promise of clarity of mind, authenticity of heart, and freedom of movement and expression. It offers a significant decrease in suffering as the need to identify or hook into any single experience or state is released.

This life which you are brings a palpable opening of channels of joy, peace, love and freedom to be of service and to express all that needs to manifest in the world. Existence is infinite in potential and it is not afraid.

Yet these expressions of humanity are the by-products of a much deeper fulfilment: the fulfilment of your purpose on this planet in human form; the fulfilment of the command: "LIVE."

This is the unifying need of every form in the universe and it could be that we are here as humanity simply for that. There is no rejection of physical form in it, only an unconditional celebration.

For a moment within the eternity of existence, we are invited to study the embodiment of life in matter, from the inside out. We are invited to meet ourselves in others. We are invited to learn through unity in manifold forms – the forms of creation.

In addition, the human form brings an incredible, slow-motion opportunity to study the interaction between three dimensions – that of mind, spirit or consciousness, associated with peace; that of sentience, being or awareness, associated with love; and that of clear perception of the physical, sentient and learning mechanisms of the universe through emptiness, associated with unity. The power to move freely through these dimensions is brought through the development of the means to realize existence as a non-dual whole, behind and integral to all perception.

From one perspective, physical life is extremely short. This is our opportunity. This life is the most important workshop we could attend. With broad brushstrokes, the process of awakening, and self-consciousness, followed by the development of awareness and culminating in the realizations of the passion born of perception through emptiness, mirrors the stages of life – from youth, young adulthood through to old age and the breakdown of the body.

This is not a religious method. Nor is it lawbreaking, anarchistic or frightening. It is a simple invitation to do more of what you are already doing: to softly open an internal inquiry through felt-experience and patient curiosity into who and what we really are.

There is no belief involved in the statement: "I exist." There is no choice in it. It is even harder to deny our existence than to deny our ultimate physical death. The thoughts and structures offered in this book are intended to support us all in surrendering to the greatest power of human life – existence itself.

4

I Exist Therefore I Exist

"We don't have to physically die to reunite with the miracle of our existence."

Through moving into our means of perception, we will invite a deeper integration between mind, heart and body. Through realizing the windows of perception, we allow the space for manifesting who we really are. This existence is so familiar when met, that illusions and entanglements release like nothing. But we don't have to physically die to reunite with the miracle of our existence.

The realization of the ways in which we perceive the world opens a process that brings greater clarity of mind, freedom from fear, and an expanded ability to allow intimacy and unity with others.

Perception is a process that works by degrees of allowance. We need to take it slowly, gently and without agenda. The more we invite and the less we push, the more we can allow the revelation of who we are.

The infinite power of this existence is such that it could explode all form, and certainly our nervous systems, yet there is a divine intelligence in creation that works with ingenious method through forms of belief and experience.

Our physical, mental, emotional and psychological structures will expand by degrees. Beliefs will not collapse, but will soften in stages until that which is no longer needed falls away – firstly like old clothes still carried behind us in a sack, and later on to be left behind and forgotten.

This is not a quick-fix process for enlightenment, but an invitation towards recognition of that which has always been here, the awesome and familiar truth of our existence in the perpetual here and now. Through this recognition, beauty sees beauty and life celebrates life – in all its manifold forms. For experienced seekers, they might notice that for all those significant experiences of awakening and enlightenment, they still find themselves with a sense of unfulfilled need. Something is not finished yet.

In blending with the inner core of this sense of lack, it is possible to open a new adventure – that in which we can move beyond experience itself into a deepening exploration of the means of perception – the windows between ourselves and the other. In this, we can begin thinning the layers between our existence and our manifestation as humans.

Between your living presence and the form of your body, mind and psychology are these wonderful windows of perception. They are windows through which we evolve. They are the openings that allow us to become fully responsive.

They are also the windows through which our existence and life can be perceived by others. If the curtains are drawn, we might begin to believe that we are forsaken and unseen, residing in the loneliness of veiled darkness, perhaps blindly waiting for the release of perception that comes with death. In this, there could be a regrettable wasted opportunity in physical time and space.

The windows of perception are the deeper structures that need to be honoured in the art of living. Freedom of perception and perspective literally means freedom to move.

When we use the word freedom, we refer to the liberation needed to become manifest as human beings.

At core, no one seeks to escape their own existence, we are all seeking to unify with it. We do not aim to transcend or escape the human, but to open the means to become super human. This is because humanity is a miracle of tremendous promise, and life is worthy of celebration.

In addition, the development and refinement of the means of perception brings an empowerment to meditation, healing, psychology, hypnotherapy, physical therapy, creativity and to any discipline where the nature of perception determines the quality of action. Its pioneers are the musicians, poets, artists and pure scientists. It will be consolidated by the academics, propagandists, marketing professionals and community voices.

We hope that the understandings here, if popularly undertaken, will lead to a refinement of a language to describe and explore together what it is to be alive. Precision of language means our communication can become more seamless – crossing the rifts that naturally divide one human form from another.

5

Liberation Through Language

"Perception does not define who we are, but it does define where we are limited."

Language has the power to change how we think and is the source of the limitations we put on our minds, hearts and direction. Through generations of habit, language has begun to define the possible, decorated with a flag that declares insanity or irrationality to those who outstep its precincts. So it is time to widen the scope of our language.

When moving into the language of the living, it is remarkable how few words come forward. Words have evolved to describe objects and fixed things, and fall poorly short of the ineffable dimension of felt experience.

As such, words are wonderful tools which can also severely limit experience. Teachers of inner growth often dance between words such as life, beauty, being, awareness, consciousness, emptiness, emotion and feeling without seeking precision, which has led to some confusion about what we are attempting to communicate.

Many talk as if we are composed of consciousness – as if this word is broad enough to describe all experience and even to stand in for existence itself. Sleep, dreaming and near-death experiences would seem to refute this.

When we refine the language of inner growth, we also open the promise of the possible.

Could it be that awareness of sentience is not only equally important as consciousness or mind, but is the source of those mental states or fear-based thinking from which we seek release?

Could it be that perception through emptiness, rather than

being a fallback position after a disappointment, shock or burnout, is actually the source of our manifesting feeling in awareness, and the attempts of consciousness to regain control through the creation of 'reality'?

Of course, we 'know' emptiness. We have all got a scent of it from the Tibetans and Zen. But have we dared to delve into it and existentially reside there through the release of all experience?

Interestingly, it seems that language itself is dormant when it comes to expressing a refinement of perception in a way that can be clearly understood, as a basis for experience and inner growth, or the language of the living.

Experienced seekers will notice that frequently the words consciousness and awareness are used interchangeably within the general sense of awakening into the present moment. In some languages, it is even hard to locate separate words.

Psychology today recognizes only consciousness for investigation, and that in itself is often debated as a source of disorder. Awareness is thrown in as an unspecified by-product of consciousness and perception through emptiness – well it's an idea that seems to have been unanimously sectioned.

In the great synergy between the mysticism of the East and the monotheism of the West, and in the synergy between differing methods of personal development or systems for spiritual attainment, something new is born. It is not either-or, it is all this.

We hope that the refinement of the language of perception offered here will be of service to the transition from perception dominated by an unawakened, temporal, lingual mind into a live synergy of perception through consciousness, awareness and emptiness, in the here and now. And the 'here' of emptiness is just as important as the 'now'.

This is a synergy that could widen the promise of freedom within human experience leading to a more fully incarnated expression of humanity.

Beyond that, this knowledge is shared because of the impact it has had on the quality of life of individuals who long felt they had reached the limits of the possible within their individual processes of inner growth.

This limit tends to be characterized by an enlightened, transcendental meta-hook into spaces which exist independently of human form, or any form. It falls short of the deepest need of all, to be free to attend to all aspect of the human body, mind, soul and spirit.

6

Suffering

"The end to suffering can only emerge after suffering itself has been fully accepted as part of the unity of creation."

Those who have a subtle agenda of escape from physical life through spirituality can reach a wall embedded in a core belief that they are defined by their suffering and by the traumatic events of their lives.

Spirituality can then take a tone of rejection of human life, which has an inevitable whiplash. In addition, increasing effort is needed to maintain the belief that this kind of enlightenment as an end point signifies an end to suffering.

The end to suffering can only emerge after suffering itself has been fully accepted as part of the unity of creation.

There is an inbuilt fault in the reflex rejection of suffering as part of present human experience. It might seem cruel to state, but at its depth suffering also has a beauty.

Freedom from the belief that suffering is permanent and the realization of its transience does not mean that suffering ceases to exist within individual or collective human experience. On the contrary, it opens a capacity for empathy and births form in the movement of compassion.

Suffering does not define who we are. It is not our creator. Our pain seems to attract us, while our well-being seems to be taken for granted. As we open the windows of perception, we might well find that a new freedom is born in which we begin to invest less in our suffering and enjoy more gratitude for the predominant well-being of the whole.

7

Spiralling Home

"Perception is actually a human window, which opens both ways."

Sitting in silence in a public place it can be remarkable to witness the imbalance between our quest outside ourselves for self-definition, purpose, identity, satisfaction, distraction or happiness, and our quest inside ourselves to explore the miraculous internal universe through which the life which is who we are is evolving at this moment.

The assertive or 'male' aspect of ourselves seems to be in overdrive, while the receptive, absorbing, allowing 'female' aspect is functioning in a default position.

This has led to an almost obsessive quest for self-definition through the material world, or through relationships. Our knowledge of the exterior world has created enough books to shroud the planet, while literature on the nature of perception – the means through which we are able to reach out and learn at all – is vastly lacking. In reflection of our collective state, perception to date is chiefly defined as perception of an individual towards the outer world.

One of the keys in this book is the suggestion that perception is actually a human window, which opens both ways. The tools offered here will impact both inner and outer experience, opening an increasing space for the embodiment of existence on all layers of form. Perception does not define who we are, but it does define where we are limited.

Yet our perception determines how we experience the outer world. It literally creates the world for us.

What is consciousness? What is awareness? How do we

perceive? How do we feel? From where does our recognition of beauty arise? How do we 'know' from a space beyond, behind or before thought? What is the process of understanding, before it is verbalized in the mind? Can it be witnessed?

Who is observing my despair when I am alone?

What are we doing here, and why, when we open our eyes in a moment of pure perception of this insane, absurd miracle of humanity in creation, do we so often close them again in pain?

When we begin to recognize and affirm the universal difference between consciousness and awareness, a new process is initiated. Already in the recognition that consciousness is not absolute, a greater space is allowed for inquiry and exploration.

Who would dare to open these windows and allow the light to come in? What would be exposed that is not ours to see? This playfulness and the perceptive inquiry into the interplay and blend between dimensions of head, heart and body is made possible through our third and most essential power of perception – that of the basis, the root, or emptiness. So often used as a barely-affirmed 'service tool' to awareness or consciousness, emptiness is the critical factor which allows any perception or creation to take place at all.

8

Allowing it All

"Why do you exist? Because I am here. Why does it matter? Because we are one."

To begin to allow perception through emptiness is to come to life in a manner which is so intimately familiar, and yet so empowering, unconditional and authentic, that a process of self-realization is initiated, through which all that has been experienced until now begins to realize itself at a depth beyond consciousness.

Emptiness is a known space, but from spaces where we are still clinging to illusions, it can look to us like hell. It is our forbidden, secret dimension. Yet when we truly fall there, we find a known sanctuary: an infinite, existential space which allows all things to exist in transition.

This is the space we go when we are thrown out of social unity, severely rejected, about to die, when we face great disappointment in all we thought we were in relation to others. Yet, it is our most private source of strength; the secret back room of our human existence; a reality behind all these attempts to be human.

When we visit it shortly and not by choice, emptiness can seem to be the harbour of intense loneliness, despair and cynicism, but it is far more than that.

It contains all that ever was, all that is and all that will ever be. In emptiness, we become apparent as indestructible existence, and this liberates us from a tremendous amount of fear.

In the realization of the transience of time, space and inner states, life itself finds an anchor in the 'here' of existence. All aspects of experience are seen with clarity, impermanent formation of atoms, thoughts and feelings. Constantly in movement, we ourselves do not move. Our body can travel from place to place, but we are not moving. Our feelings rush in, develop and transform, but we are not changing. Our thoughts busily seek definition, structure, or safety, but we have no need of any of this.

Why do you exist? Because I am here. Why does it matter? Because we are here.

You can never get lost in the emptiness, or in any other space or dimension you chose to reclaim. There is always a spiralling motion in which life recalls itself in a movement of inner unification through all the dimensions of human being, living and doing. Even total chaos is witnessed and seen. Even the breakdown of all our forms is observed. We are that which timeless both witnesses and observes. That which is: manifesting through it all.

In order to move into perception through emptiness, we need to allow what is present in our lives and experience to exist in its entirety. There needs to be an inner decision to no longer keep secrets – especially from ourselves. This requires a dedication of self-inquiry, and a great deal of courage and honesty.

What is this? What is this rage, this fear, this love? Who is this, perceiving it all, through battle, boredom or through bliss? Who is creating and destroying? Who is the author of this life I am composing?

Through the allowance of thoughts, sensations, feeling and emotion, we are able to create space between the object of distress or pleasure and the window of perception. The trilogy of perception brings the tools of inquiry through which we can move more deeply into that which essentially perceives, unhooked from the object which is perceived. This is a process of unfolding back to the source of life, or of coming to life. In inner growth, it is known as moving beyond duality – away from the split of subject (the one that is seeing) and object (that which is seen), to an inclusive location in existence itself.

Those same teachings often identify this location as pure awareness (when awareness becomes aware of itself), but it is even more inclusive than that. The perceptive existence that arises in emptiness does not bring anyone perspective of location. It brings total non-dual unity in the recognition of all states as non-separate emanations of itself. This brings the freedom of choice of perspective to the dimension or area most attuned to the needs of the moment.

The development of consciousness opens our capacity to truly know life from dimensions of serenity and silence.

The development of awareness allows us to feel the manifold layers of experience beyond polarity as our qualities manifest through essential being.

Perception through emptiness is that which liberates the three means of perception to move in an increasing blend. Through this allowance, experience itself becomes less relevant than the miracle of that which is able to experience through all the layers.

It starts here, right now, with you.

9

Beauty of the Unborn

"The core basis of our experience as human beings, through transitions of life and death, is with you now, in this moment."

All that exists is within the now – beyond linear time. As such, the core basis of our experience as human beings is with us in this moment. Our physical death is not a future event, it is now. Our conception is not a past event, it is also present in the now. The ordering of these events is only a function of physical time, not of sentient time or linear time. Our mortality is ever present.

Therefore, in exploring perception, it is good to look at our origins – to sense a little of what was there before our conception – whether or not we chose to believe in life before birth.

It seems that we have a constant on-call access to the infinite universal resources of peace, love and unity. So inherent are these to all that we know and experience as human beings, that we could almost forget they are there as an aspect of existence.

Yet the backdrop to hatred is love.

For some, these universal aspects could be called the soul. For others, there is logic to these dimensions of human experience which is free of belief. Even if we are nothing more than a human brain processing all this input of its attachment to an animal body, the same experience can be described as an existential part of our psychological make-up.

What were we before we found ourselves physically alive in the great light show of learning, feeling and manifestation? Before we were conceived, or in the moment of conception of new life, what was around us?

Before we were conceived, before this physical thing happened in which sperm collided with egg deep inside the cervical canal of the mother, there was peace. Whether or not we believe in life before birth, it was peaceful. There was no polarity. Yet there was a movement, a passion vibrating through the stillness, a passion or need for life.

Before we were conceived, whether or not we believe in life before birth, there was love. This love was pervading through the plane of divided forms, blending, attracting, and moving male and female, sperm and egg towards collision. If we think there was not love between our parents, then there was attraction which meant that these bodies came together in union to create a new form.

In the moment we were conceived, whether or not we believe in life before birth, there was a new unity created, emerging from the indivisible emptiness. This new unity, containing physical and energetic particles of both father and mother, is the first cell of who we are in this moment.

In the creation of form, this unity remains the container to the accelerating division of cell from cell which is the physical expression of life becoming manifest.

As such, at the depths of who we are, there are some living core components. There is a soulful backdrop of love and peace. There is an ultimate container of unity, dividing itself through creation to a new, relative unity. There is a stress and sensuality of creation as it happens, and male and female come into blend through sexual union. And there is existence: a manifesting droplet of life.

At the moment of conception, these aspects are all there; separately yet indivisibly part of a whole. Peace, love and unity; activity, receptivity, stillness; creation, division and a new unity: the infinite resources of our universe in magnificent interplay with life itself, the existential you.

Right now, you are alive in that, at the same time that you are physically and mentally here, reading the words on this page.

10

Human

"The opening of the eyes of existence in the midst of the commonplace, beyond all our aspirations and dreams, brings the fundamental building blocks of the miraculous."

Somewhere planted deep in the universe is a powerful seed – a seed found at the basis of every human being and every atom. It is the seed of creation, and of evolution.

It is the seed at the basis of every scientist and mathematician that slaves late into the night with the endless curiosity to understand our objective universe. It is the seed behind the passion of innovators – to make things better – if not for others then for a sense of self-fulfilment.

It is the seed implanted at the basis of every artist and every musician. It is that which within millennia of human striving seeks to create a better world, just because it is there and we comprehend and know that it is possible. In a way, this essential seed has one command: "Grow."

At the junction between time and space, life and body and at the intersection of our individual existence with the existence of others, there is a second seed. Beyond thought and mind, at the basis of felt experience, this seed expresses the command: "Be."

At the heights of our existence in individual human form, there is a third seed. Behind every choice, thought and creation, from birth until death, the command of this pure existential spirit is "Know." This is a seed that contains and runs through all aspects of living, being and evolution.

The fullest expression of who we are – growing, being and knowing – involves opening the three dimensions of human – through the perceptive means of emptiness, awareness and consciousness.

Loyalty to these existential commands requires a certain alchemy which arises from an attitude of acceptance. It is not surprising that the first step in the 12-step program for addiction is to acknowledge a higher power. Acknowledgment that the individual identity or qualities or experience is not separate from the united field of human endeavour is critical in allowing manifestation. To pretend to be alone in this is simply to pretend.

From shared fields of collective consciousness, through to the perfect tuning of awareness (for example, at a musical performance), through to the shared vibrations of the planet and tides moving through every physical form, we are one. We are one, yet we remain individually precious, special and unique at the same time.

In order to truly allow the manifestation of the individual purpose, being and knowledge, it is necessary to release the idea that the individual is ultimately separate from the whole.

On the level of mind, thinking and consciousness, we need to learn to "Let it fall". This means to develop a capacity to drop our thoughts or our thinking processes and to allow consciousness to perceive directly without the stained glass of linguistic thinking.

On the level of the heart, feeling or awareness, we need to "Let it be". This means to purely allow whatever emotions or feelings that are arising to be invited with openness and to authentically allow them into our experience – observing them as a gardener observes the flowering of his garden.

On the level of the physical body, existence or emptiness, we need to "Be for real". When we search for experience or elevated states, or seek distraction through pleasure or even pain, we are often blocking our raw existence. The opening of the eyes of existence in the midst of the commonplace, beyond all our aspirations and dreams, brings the fundamental building blocks of the miraculous.

II

Consciousness

"The reflection of a reflection of a reflection of pure light."

I

Out of the Mind

"Inherent in this linguistic ability to think is to lie."

The great 'I' towering with the power and authority of social consensus and law is our fishing rod in the world of human interaction. Through the 'I' we define ourselves: firstly, with our physical body and birth name, and later, with whole structures of identity.

Early on, we learn that our parents and the world have demands of us, for better or worse. We are demanded to be 'good' and to not be 'bad'. The price of falling on the wrong side of such judgement is rejection. As a helpless child, the risk of rejection is too high, so often we begin to strategize an acceptable persona at a young age. We invest this protective self with consciousness, giving it life. We defend it as if it were alive. Yet all the time, we consciously witness from a greater 'I': that which sees the changes in the body as the child becomes a teenager; that which witnesses the composition of personality, and the early formation of a life plan.

When we lose connection with the unhooked 'I', the tool which we engage with form, and with the one who is the master of that tool, then we lose our freedom and can become caught in our own webs of identity as if they were absolute.

Consciousness seems to be the height of our evolution. Unlike the animal kingdom, humans have the advanced ability to use language, to think with the mind, and to communicate.

Inherent in this linguistic ability to think is to lie. The word dog does not actually have any absolute link with the form which is a dog. In the same way, the stories we compose about our reality are not tied in any absolute way to this object named 'reality'.

This kind of reality is at most a reflective description of an experience which has passed. It is always relative, and never true in any absolute sense. Yet this linguistic ability of consciousness to define experience, locate cause and effect, and communicate wisdom is not to be thrown away. It is a powerful tool that needs to remain an instrument at our command, not a dictator of our living experience.

The ability to make good use of our minds is connected with our ability to freely invest thoughts and forms with our consciousness, thus giving them a kind of life, and our equal ability to disinvest – to unhook consciousness from the thought patterns or thinking habits. For this, consciousness needs to be free. It is a window of perception, over which we must realize that we have the great responsibility of being the master.

While all aspects of living experience are processed through the brain, this does not mean that they are initiated there. The brain does its best job to keep balance and preserve the organism, with all the information available. It is a physical headquarters of integration and human existence, but it is responsive, not absolute. In this, it can send signals back to the rest of human experience, based on learning, such as "Don't look to your left on a rainy day because you might bump into a lamp post." But these signals are based on programming and do not need to become beliefs, judgement and laws if we are able to honour the consciousness that gives the brain its power.

2

Awakening

"To awaken is to know we have been asleep, asleep in our living."

When consciousness becomes conscious of consciousness – existence can come as a shock – sometimes with a sense of surrealism. "How did I come to be in this job, with this partner, in this country?" How did I forget that this is who I am? Such experiences are commonly referred to as spiritual awakening. It is a refreshing awakening which creates space when we turn back – as we will – to readdress the world of form: habits, thought patterns and emotional entanglements. It creates an opportunity for liberation or purification from those parts of daily life which are no longer serving our highest interests.

Often, the opening of consciousness can occur through the faculty of the visual, through 'seeing'.

You are cleaning the kitchen, as you do every night. At the same time, you are thinking about your day, or perhaps some emotional entanglements. You are looking at your hands, covered with soap. Your hands are moving by themselves. You look at the form, perceiving these hands you have known your whole life as they operate. A memory comes forward of soap bubbles as a child. Yet here you are now, still with the same existence in a grown body. I have grown older, yet I have not changed. A miracle of existence can break through – from a space beyond the thinking mind.

An awakening can also be triggered by a growing mindfulness or sudden disentanglement from the absurdity of thought patterns or emotional habits. "I want to be free of I" or "I hate myself" can trigger such a break in the habitual conscious

39

state of the internal inner fight. Who is the "I" who hates who?

You are already a master of your own consciousness, and at any moment can choose to take hold of the reins. This is accomplished by accepting that consciousness is just a window – it is not who we are. It is one means through which we perceive the world as humans. When neglected, this perception itself can be dirtied by judgment, beliefs and fears of rejection. These distortions can affect the way we experience ourselves, our world, and the way we relate to others.

Through emptiness, we can take the 'seeing is believing' of consciousness, and make it 'seeing is not believing', which releases consciousness to a greater expansion of possibility. All we can ever perceive through our consciousness is our particular perspective in time, space and spiritual development.

Each awakening into consciousness also demands integration with the state of 'normal' life. Liberated consciousness brings the possibility to choose how deeply we want to reattach to the current beliefs or habitual patterns of the thinking mind. Yet the more we are awakened, the less absolute the investment of consciousness in thoughts, beliefs and 'realities' becomes. We become players of illusion that serve the highest good. We become more honest. No such truth is absolute.

3

Qualities of Consciousness

"If we have been abused, manipulated or dominated, there could be a reluctance to accept the arbitrary power of consciousness."

Consciousness is sharp, alert and its space of energetic initiation is in the centre of the head. It can be directed to any part of the body, physically or in terms of inner feelings. It is closely connected with control.

An imbalance in conscious assertion or the ability to receive the consciousness of another is reflected in the eyeballs – and as such, energetic exercises that include balancing right and left eye are helpful in centring and concentration. The moment we really 'see' with our eyes the perceptive window of consciousness is opening.

When we move behind the habitual thinking mind and consciousness becomes conscious of itself, there can be a rapid chain reaction which brings us swiftly into the power of the now and into an experience – albeit momentary – of freedom from all that is presently limiting us – whether in mind, body or soul.

When actively opened as a window of perception, consciousness carries a lot of light and as such is powerful, creating charisma and generating authority. It can be used on others for domination – as many will shy away from the full consciousness of another – as it awakens a kind of instinctive shame or fear of intimacy. As such, the experience of abuse or 'brainwash' of the 'reality' can lead to a fear to truly espouse the power of consciousness, lest harm is inflicted on others.

In opening the window of consciousness to greater degrees, we need to inquire into issues of authority and responsibility.

These are the gatekeepers of this portal of perception. If we have been abused, manipulated or dominated, there could be a reluctance to accept the arbitrary power of consciousness. This is a loss – because when mastered, consciousness can invest the world with freedom and promise; it no longer needs to be a dictator of the truth to others.

In addition, the power of consciousness is so much part of our make-up, that the attempt to avoid it can lead to the uncontrolled emergence of a separate personality: the mouse can suddenly and unexpectedly become a dictator, as the power of consciousness is unwittingly released with a vengeance by fear or threat.

The connection between consciousness and power or authority can mean that some tend to avoid perception through consciousness. Out of fear of taking authority which could equate them with the 'bad' guy, some can shy from the affirmative portal of consciousness and choose to rather drift in a flow of awareness. The imbalance can make it hard to take decisions, or to plan and structure daily life.

Whatever our story, or the imprint of our experience, we are responsible for the window of consciousness. It is one of the perceptive means which brings us security, self-definition and 'remembering' of that which has been pushed into the land of shadows. This means that to heal the damage done by the abuse of consciousness, we need to reclaim our perceptive window, even if this means moving through the fear and cruelty present in the interpersonal formulas of abuse.

Alternatively, those on the other side of the abuse polarity, who have routinely used consciousness in order to support a position of power, status, or domination, might find themselves dictating their own experience, and becoming lost in an increasing web of pretence. They deny the perceived helplessness of the receptive window of awareness in order to control and manipulate the living, feeling and emotional aspects of human experience according to the convenience of the mind. The constant need to dictate reality and to defend truth against the 'other' can lead to obsession, paranoia, self-pity and loneliness. It is also an imbalance driven by survival fears.

When consciousness is driven by a fear to survive and not by a deeper wisdom of affinity with love, peace and unity, this imbalance can become a significant cause of suffering.

4

Divide and Multiply

"In this world of creative illusion, nothing lasts forever. Nothing is the backdrop to all illusion."

Consciousness makes choices. When you choose to focus on the left, you are not looking to the right. The right is rejected. When you structure your reality, you cut off pieces from the whole. When you assert your authority – that is, your own inherent authorship of your own story – you could be negating the truth of another. Worse than that, when we move with consciousness, we could make mistakes and be held accountable.

It is therefore necessary to have some peace with an inner permission to make mistakes, honouring the beauty of processes of learning rather than cleaving to illusions of perfection. A degree of humility, wisdom and responsibility is needed for consciousness to be truly opened.

Consciousness, as an aspect of living, has the ability to divide. When we become more conscious, we create a spatial border between ourselves and others – which is good when there is a need for this. We become conscious of a separate body, of separate senses, and separate experience and perspective.

Individual consciousness tends to lead to a place of unity in which we become godlike, the power source of our own universe, able to create and destroy our reality at will; and yet in that, it can leave us deeply immersed in a sense of our own separation or solitude. In this world of creative illusion, nothing lasts forever. Indeed, nothing is the backdrop to all illusion.

In itself, consciousness could drive us 'insane'. We could not be physically alive without the added portal of emptiness and the critical junction of awareness which softly holds experience in momentary form. It would also be impossible to integrate the light of consciousness alone into the body, still less to structure our minds, thoughts, experience or daily lives.

To put it bluntly, if we were only dwelling through consciousness, we would never sleep, with all the physical, psychological and mental consequences of that. The evidence of sleep and unconscious states should have been enough to encourage the wisdom of the relativity of consciousness.

Consciousness is energetically initiated in the centre of the head and in the brain. As such, it is intimately connected with the five physical senses: sight, hearing, touch, taste and smell. It also has a powerful connection with the region of the solar plexus – the energetic dimension of fear, freedom and social relations.

Consciousness sets boundaries. The moment we come into bodily consciousness, our body claims its separate space. I am not you. The moment we move our consciousness to our thoughts and beliefs, we put light on them and own them as individual.

It is important to note that while conscious perception is initiated at the centre of the head, consciousness, like the experience of awareness or perception through emptiness, is a power that is multidimensional and expansive. Consciousness can expand its lens to cover a whole defined area; and it can evolve through a blend with awareness and emptiness.

Imagine again the windows in our three-story castle. When you draw close to the window, the view fills your whole perception. So it is with consciousness, such that it can also contain all three layers – from the infinite sky to the undulating earth.

As a natural movement, consciousness seems to prefer to divide itself into substations. It can separate itself into satellites across experience, or distribute itself to focus on key spots of the body (for example, the bottom of the feet when walking without shoes). The primary witness of consciousness can scatter into whole units of sub-witnesses.

We can maintain a conscious satellite in an area of the body where we have pain. If we are rejecting the pain, then a substation of consciousness can be maintained to repress or 'normalize' the experience and thus form an energetic block.

This can often be the case with unwanted anger or fear, or denial of helplessness in challenging circumstances such as during a process of loss or grief.

There is nothing wrong with this as consciousness functions first and foremost to support survival – to keep us on our feet, literally – but at some stage the same consciousness will need to allow the healing of the rifts it has created – especially when they in turn begin to threaten our survival. This is found in the critical ability surrender attachment, to unhook the sub-witnesses and to call them home.

The separated parts of our energy system will do what they need to survive – recruiting the consciousness needed for this. Yet in every division, a pressure is created. At some stage, blocks can explode and the satellites will return to source or the greater witness – bringing a crisis and an opportunity to heal the area of rejection that created the wound or block in the first place.

Such spiritual journeys can occur through small incidents, lifetime processes around specific themes, or both. The end point is always reintegration and unity.

You can use consciousness to open your heart, and likewise use it to shield the heart. As such, the deployment of consciousness is an active part of the expression of free will. We can invest a thought with consciousness with such strength that it seems to gain a life and autonomy of its own. With consciousness, we are co-creators of realities, for better or worse. The abuse of consciousness in creating reality according to a wounded agenda can manifest in forms of psychopathy or other personality disorders. Yet the worst suffering is always within the fear-driven individual who increasingly needs to compose mask after mask of appearance – masks which can lead to a deep feeling of isolation and being unseen by others.

As with thoughts, so it is with emotions. The use of consciousness can create energetic blocks – for example, in order to encase, deny or hide some anger, fear or shame.

Alive with the investment, these conscious automatons (or blocks) begin to dictate the thought patterns, activating the mind to gain the needed input of consciousness to sustain their autonomous life.

This is why the attention is so often attracted to precisely the places where you are suffering. When there is a lack of freedom in the dimension of consciousness, you can find yourself increasingly defined by suffering, and a story in which a biography of pain gives form to your life, or even seems to give a right to exist.

5

Wake-up Calls

"Silence is not a dormant space. It is the dimension in which our consciousness comes to life."

At certain moments in life, consciousness takes a step back from thought processes and moves to a transcendental position regardless of choice. This is a natural movement which allows the mind to adjust to change.

It can happen suddenly, after a shock or trauma, or as a result of mental breakdown, or it can happen more subtly. When consciousness frees itself of the determination of thought by becoming conscious of itself, we gain an opportunity to reset the self-identity (for example, from "I am Daddy's little girl" to "I am a pensioner"!). We have a chance to recompose ourselves.

Yet we do not have to wait for the inevitable awakenings. It is possible at any moment to become aware of verbal thoughts, of the chattering voices in the back of the mind, or of inherent silence, the prevalent space between and behind all thoughts.

By turning attention to the space between thoughts, we can allow the freedom of spaciousness to emerge between existence, and the thoughts circling in the head.

We do not need to interfere with thinking, but by attending to where the thoughts are not happening, we will find they begin to lose their absolute grip. As the originating earth of thought, the silence is always more powerful. All we need to do is allow it to coexist with all activity.

Silence is not a dormant space. It is the dimension in which our consciousness comes to life.

6

Consciousness and Free Will

"Thoughts based on avoiding danger in the past can today become thoughts that hold our life hostage to the dictates of fear."

In the dimension of consciousness, the world seems to be full of choices. You can choose to put this book down and never look at it again. You can make conscious choices to never drive down a certain street, never talk to a certain person, to hunt a person or thing that we want, to lie and to trust.

The practice of making conscious choices is a good way to begin realizing the freedom and playfulness expressed behind free will. This freedom will turn out to be far more important to you than the consequences of any one decision. It is freedom of mind and the freedom of perspective which can open the fulfilment of living.

You can choose to believe in your thoughts and to invest them with definitive power over who you are. Yet in that kind of choice, we actually lose the freedom to choose.

If we choose to allow our thoughts to define us, then our thoughts become the ones choosing, according to immediate gratification. We become slaves to a reactive sequence which is often based on fear.

The deeper freedom of choice comes from a space where all thoughts and possibilities can exist.

When we are drugged or half-asleep, we walk blindly behind others in their direction. In the same way, our habitual thoughts and our structures of belief based on conditioning, culture, or painful experience anaesthetise our deeper freedom to choose. Thoughts based on avoiding danger in the past, can today become the thoughts that hold our life hostage to the dictates of fear.

Out of 'free' will, we could find ourselves choosing to justify deep layers of depression in our vitality and well-being. This justification, arising from the need to be 'OK', begins to take form as a belief. For a belief to stand, we often feel a need to project it on others. Our personal state of depression becomes a universal truth. This can create quite an aggression and distrust towards others who dare to be happy. We know better: "It will end in tears." We rejoice when they suffer, as our belief is affirmed.

Our beliefs play an important role in structuring this freedom of choice. Some beliefs support our processes of change and inner growth, while others can increasingly become like prisons which shrink by degrees. As such, it is good that beliefs should be treated with softness, as entities which are evolving according to the highest need.

Free will is a gift of consciousness. But we need to be willing to accept that gift.

Within the realm of experience, the most we can do is to work with transformation, which requires an interactive synergy of the trilogy of perceptive powers. We can freeze our anger or fear; we can choose fixation over fluidity and we can choose to cling to form rather than surrender to the risk of change.

But we do not have the freedom to deny consciousness. It will wait for us until we are ready, no matter how long that takes. This freedom is intrinsically connected to our pure life or existence. We cannot make existence go away. We have no right NOT to exist.

7

Conscious Inquiry

"As consciousness is liberated, we can experience complete layers of false self."

For consciousness to open, it must be ready to surrender itself, in a receptive moment in which we allow it to unhook from thoughts, feelings, objects, experiences or states of being. When we let consciousness surrender control over our identity, we move to a position where we are observing consciousness itself. This is a great step towards freedom.

Within this freedom, consciousness can trace a thought or form to its root source or cause – its place of origin. For example, the origin of a compulsive argument in the head against the neighbour could be a deep need to be affirmed in the right to exist in physical form on the planet.

Sometimes, we can dialogue with a whole sub-personality which in itself has become invested with its own consciousness. Though inner communication, it is possible to negotiate the core intent of the separated part. Often this is born of pain, isolation or abandonment, and its direction is towards love, peace and unity. In recognizing the shared core intent of sub-personalities, reintegration is made possible for the empowerment and clarification of the field of consciousness as a whole.

As the inherent intent of phenomenon becomes clearer, life itself can satiate the need for irreproachable existence, silencing the need for the inner fight. In this kind of situation we can observe how consciousness can allow the thought, problem or issue back into the overall field, just by first of all unhooking it from life and allowing observation or mindfulness.

As consciousness is liberated, we can become conscious of

complete layers of false self. In allowing the existential separation from this 'one' (who we have been, and who we have never been), we can welcome it home. The prior self is absorbed into a more authentic layer of self-hood or human manifestation.

This is a process made possible through conscious inquiry. "Who is this one that is jealous?" Can you find her? "Who is this one who feels neglected?" Where does he live?

As we become more empowered through the liberation of consciousness from a fixed investment in form, a deeper form of conscious control emerges – one which is a more authentic expression of human wholeness. In addition, we gain one of the greatest tools of human living – the power of authentic inquiry.

8

Project Me Not

"In a sense, we are all children to one another, and as such should move with the peacefulness, softness and respect towards the authenticity of another's experience."

Consciousness is also the power behind our ability to project. Classically, teachers have talked about the movie theatre. Experience is projected by consciousness on the screen. We are not the movie which flickers there, it is argued; and rather, we should realize the inherent quality of the screen on which all movies occur.

This is true, but it could be added that we are also the projector itself and the one which selects the film of a lifetime. From the perspective of existence, we can leave the whole movie hall. And even if it is not our wish to leave, it is important to remember that the theatre does not limit us.

But in meantime, it is necessary to look at the way we project. This is because our projections, without responsibility, not only affect our state, but also have an impact on others in the unified web of humanity.

It has often been observed that those aspects which enrage us so much in the other tend to be aspects that are unresolved within ourselves.

These disowned energetic blocks can seem to be 'other' – no longer a part of who we are, at least not of who we decide we are. Yet we continue to be attracted to precisely those areas of blockage. We still want to study this horror, cruelty or suffering, preferably on the screen of another human being, or at least on the latest crime program on TV.

So determined are we in our wounded agenda to disown

some thoughts, feelings or emotions, that we verbally or energetically launch them towards other human beings – in the form of projection.

In this manner, some of us create whole novellas of good versus evil by projecting such inner fights onto the tabula rasa of the life of the other. The less we actually allow the inherent existence of the other and of ourselves, the easier it becomes to do this.

This is destructive enough when verbalized, but such projections can also have a cruel energetic impact on another person – especially if they are vulnerable (for example, our own children). Children tend to have a deep wish to please their parents, and as such will comply with the parental projections – if this is what they feel will keep a sense of peace, love and unity. Yet often, it creates the opposite as the parent sees the child acting out their own worst nightmares.

In a sense, we are all children to one another, and as such should move with the greatest love, softness and respect towards the authenticity of another's experience.

9

Consciousness and Will Power

"It is important to inquire into the purity of our intention, on a regular basis."

For many who have experienced awakening on the upper plane of consciousness, and found the way to move into stillness, the question returns: "Why am I still suffering?"

There is no doubt that from birth until death, consciousness is an initiator and power source of perception. It can focus in a tremendous presence, expand through different dimensions, and charge any individual cell, body part, thought or emotion with pure vitality.

As the awakening aspect, it has the ability to allow or deny whole aspects of experience. It is a creator and destroyer, a gatekeeper of unity and an instigator of division.

It is the perceptive power that can issue orders for war or for peace. It is the existential censor that manipulates and structures beliefs. It can include and respect, and/or it can deny and reject. And it does this according to a deeper will – beyond itself.

This will or intention could be formed out of trauma, pain or pure instinct to protect, or it can manifest in alignment with a collective will to evolve through creation. As such it is important to inquire into the purity of our intention, on a regular basis.

10

Consciousness and Humility

"If we were built as pyramid in creation, then consciousness would be the top stone."

In some mystical traditions and schools of psychology, 'consciousness' is used as an absolute term for life. It defines a general state of alertness: being awake, or being receptive to stimuli. The opposite would be sleep: either physical sleep or waking sleep.

All that which has not fully entered the light networks of mind or brain tends to be classed as unconscious or subconscious. Yet it is in the 'black box' of the unconscious where much of the manifestation of existence occurs.

If we were built as pyramid in creation, then consciousness would be the top stone. Without the basis of awareness and material reality or emptiness, it would collapse. As such the predominance given to consciousness, mind and brain reflects a deep experiential misunderstanding of the workings of perception. A problem at the basis or in the body will reflect through awareness, instinct or feeling, which in turn will trigger a process within consciousness. Consciousness might be on top, but it is not superior. It is fundamentally interdependent on the whole.

Within some schools of inner growth – many inspired by a Westernized intake of the mystical traditions of India – consciousness is prioritized as the central aspect of spiritual development and the 'freeing' of consciousness from thoughts, ego and emotions as a main goal and end point of spiritual development. It is important to realize that the word consciousness here is a translation for perception in general – in a manner not refined to different windows of perception. If our aim was to transcend human life, then it would make nonsense of why we are here as human beings at all. And anyway, we are here. A major role of consciousness within the trilogy of perception is in the area of empowerment. Any process, wound, block or thought pattern will become quickened by moving consciousness towards it. It has a heat and it brings life and form. This is fine, as long as we continue to take responsibility for our creations from the liberated position of existence behind consciousness.

Any experience, accompanied by an opening of greater consciousness, will become more vital, more intense and more compelling. Yet the more alive or energized the thought form becomes, the more it becomes clear from a place of witnessing that this is not what we are. The separate vitality itself can facilitate freedom.

As we master consciousness, we can even use its power to explode blocks or certain patterns, or to put in transient but powerful borders of protection, but this is only needed in certain situations, and can occur quite naturally.

11

Doing Time

"Time is something we are doing. It does not define us."

Consciousness can unhook itself from experience and exist in freedom in the present moment. We can be conscious of consciousness of consciousness of consciousness. It is a liberating and invigorating experience. This is pure vitality. It brings immediate relief from emotion, feeling, physical pain, thoughts, beliefs, agony or guilt that routinely define our state: a taste of heaven – for a moment.

Part of the liberating effect of unhooking conscious attachments is that the cause of much of our suffering is found in linear time. There is a tendency to give the organization of time into past, present and future an absolute status. This is supported by what we witness as processes of cause and effect. However, while linear time is important, it always excludes us. It is finite and limited. We only get a bit of it. Then we are cancelled out. Therefore, the belief in the absolute nature of linear time will always bring a tremendous sense of lack and dissatisfaction.

Beyond that, this organization of time is a functional projection. It is an aspect of linguistic or mental organization which facilitates manifestation. It is a technique for living, but it does not define life. Time is something we are doing as humans. It does not define who we are.

Fear and its resulting disorder anxiety is hooked into an imagined event or series of events which 'could' happen in an imaginary future – a future projected by our minds. This projection is often formed on the basis of events that happened in the past, where aspects of us were broken off in order to survive.

Fear in the present moment will only ever be relevant to the grounded threat of the present moment, which when it is not physical is open to investigation.

A great deal of complicated suffering is a function of linear time – relating to what was or what might be. It is a product of memory – both what the psychologists would term cognitive memory (the chronological series of events) and emotional memory (the memory of events in the terms of how they made us feel). Cognitive memory can be healed through remembering on the level of the mind and consciousness. Emotional memory works through enlightening and recalling frozen energy on the level of sentience and awareness.

The practice of coming into the 'now' – especially in the midst of intense experience or entanglement – is critical to the movement which takes the challenge of being human and turns it into an authentic opportunity. The now brings an immediate relativity to the structures of the thinking mind and allows a perspective which is in itself free of cause and effect.

Consciousness, when unhooked from thoughts, is able to bring us this freedom. It can also allow the opening of awareness and emotional memory – the episodes of sentient regression which can be needed to conclude chapters of our lives and release unnecessary fears for the future.

The return to the present moment, to the here and now, is inherent to processes of inner growth at every stage. Meditation takes place in the Now. Mindfulness is an experience of the Now; as is the expansion of awareness; or the existential perception through emptiness. Now is all there is.

The simplest and safest sanctuary in the present moment is to become present in the physical body – in a conscious space undetermined by thoughts of future or past.

This body is right now your container, and by coming into consciousness of the body, you can create an opportunity for deeper embodiment. This is important, as the tools offered in this book are intended to support the miracle of creation, or human life, not to create an escape from human responsibility.

Humans are strange creatures in that they would rather expand their suffering into ever-increasing webs of mental and energetic agony than suffer the pain in its raw, living form for a moment and let it pass. This is connected to our inborn instinct to preserve form. This instinct becomes confused as existence begins to manifest through the physical. Very early on, we develop a core belief that being physical means that we could cease to exist, along with the body.

Perhaps it needs to be taken on trust, but it seems that the body is a limitation on existence, not a generator of it. It is a limitation needed, like a safe classroom, for us to pursue an inquiry into the greatest powers of the universe.

Through the need to care for form and preserve it, we can neglect the existence from which form was born, confusing the manifestation for that which is manifesting. As such, we can become crowded with forms which are no longer needed. In our struggle to survive life, we begin to kill it off, moment by moment.

We swaddle ourselves with endless, lesser sufferings in order to numb the feared pain of living experience. This state begins to feel like home – it becomes an illusion of 'safety'. So we invest in it, gathering more raw material until it starts to grow by itself as a forest of thorns around the very place where no suffering can be found – existence itself.

Yet by leveraging the present moment to transcend these somewhat autonomous systems of our minds, we can find we are able to experience a space of pure light, a space where we are not defined by traumatized decisions taken long ago in the idea of our past.

In this space, we exist as a miracle that allows all experience and yet which is, in itself, greater than all that. We can experience a moment (or perhaps many moments) of freedom.

As we begin opening the windows of perception, we can

experience an acceleration of awakening. The rare experience of the Now increases in frequency, reflecting a quickening of the entire energy system. The door to the Now is opened with the release of consciousness from identification with form. The form, thought or feeling is there, but it no longer has autocratic rule over experience. Other possibilities emerge.

Within an effective process of inner growth, what was once NOW (a year passes) becomes NOW (a month passes) and accelerates to NOW, NOW, NOW (second by second).

At a certain stage, the NOW can dissolve, as it expands to an eternal dimension behind time yet ever present within our lives. You have moved to a space that coexists behind this lifetime.

12

Active: Penetration

"When there is an urgency to be heard, or to bring people together, then consciousness is an important tool to initiate and amplify the message."

Everything alive has an element of push, pull and still; or active, receptive and purely perceptive.

With sword-like power, active consciousness has the quality of penetration when it is deliberately cultivated and asserted.

When we focus with consciousness on an object, we not only empower it, we can also overwhelm it with a light. In this, the 'being' of the rock can awaken and begin to sing its story. In this, the empowerment of consciousness means we can initiate new levels of vibration in the material and energetic world, and in others.

To physically touch another consciously means we are able to bring the pure alertness and sensitivity of alertness to the felt experience at the point of contact.

We can channel consciousness from the centre of the head and bring it completely to the tiniest particle of sensation at the interface of touch. Through a satellite of consciousness, we can 'become' the space of contact. In this intense focussing, nothing else exists. We become the eyes, ears, taste, and touch at the space of choice. It can become the universe.

Within the healing arts, this can bring insight into the local area, at the same time that it unlocks a localized expansion of awareness facilitated by emptiness. It is a strong tool, and its use is specific to need. It can create a sudden energetic release which can cause the other person's body to physically jump. It can explode a block, but because in its pure form it is less organic and holistic than the use of awareness, the block will sometimes reform itself. The consciousness of the client also draws on the same infinite source.

The generation of the ability to move with active consciousness is a powerful tool in areas where we need to take on power or authority. Some will shy from this as power, authority and charisma can seem almost 'dirty'. The shame which leads us to shy from this could be because the responsibility of power terrifies us as we are not yet able to truly take responsibility for living.

It can also be fearful to go there, as this kind of power – the power generated by an intense consciousness – can also frequently appear as megalomaniac, egocentric, self-serving and dangerous. These are all areas where we could have been wounded as children.

In this structure, the conscious one dominates, and the 'crowd' must either receive the message or reject. The strongest consciousness recklessly dictates the 'truth' at any given point of space and time. This truth polarizes into an 'in-or-out, with me or against me' structure.

Yet when there is an urgency to be heard, or to bring people together, or when anyway we are given the responsibility of teacher or leader, then consciousness is an important tool to initiate and amplify the message. The polarizing effect can be ameliorated by the message, and by an invitation to engage in conscious discussion.

An open heart and receptive awareness will always be available to support unity when an increase in consciousness comes into play.

If we come into conscious collision with an authority, we do not need to capitulate. Consciousness comes from an infinite source, and as such is available to us beyond limits of life and death to set the necessary borders.

13

Receptive: Centring

"This is the space of active listening."

When it moves with receptivity, consciousness settles at the energetic headquarters at the centre of the head. This position also generates a high degree of presence and a good deal of authority. This is the space of active listening.

When we develop the capacity to be in this position of centred, receptive consciousness – which is not actively structuring, deciding or creating – then we create an invitation to the conscious expression of the other...

Conscious receptivity does not receive more noise, it issues an invitation to existence to manifest. This involves a clearance of the active habit of hooking into words, what is said, and what is thought. The need to communicate our own individuality is put aside with an invitation for information or perspectives from the outside to be revealed.

When we find ourselves and our consciousness scattered, it can be worthwhile to take a few seconds to centre ourselves through moving our consciousness into receptivity by withdrawing our energy to focus from the third eye to the centre of the head. In a crisis, it is often a reflex, and it is a reflex that can be cultivated so that the movement becomes more natural.

The practice of mindfulness – of being mindful of the breathing in and out as it travels into the body and out again – without interfering with feelings, thoughts or emotions that we meet there – is also a powerful healing and centring tool of receptive consciousness.

14

Still: Silence

"The attendance which is beyond agenda"

From a human perspective, much of what is apparent is often obscured. We can wander around, indoors and outside, with an unquestioned assumption that the blue sky above us is a container or a ceiling over our world. It is not. It is infinite. Equally, it can be felt that our world is full of noise – outside of our heads, inside our heads, across cyberspace and TV – an endless cacophony of articulation. In truth, the vast majority of our experience on the planet is happening in the presence of the depths of silence.

When consciousness is free, we are able to move into a dimension where thoughts are no longer of any purpose other than to function, structure, understand and communicate. In this state of the stillness of silence, we are supported by a backdrop of peace and disentanglement which is far more powerful than the transient activity of the thinking mind.

An infinite, unentangled dimension of spaciousness is opened for contemplation and meditation through which it is increasingly possible to be still with others – even by attending to the silence between and behind their words. The stillness of silence is not the alternative to noise. It is neither active nor receptive; neither talking nor inquiring. It is the attendance which is beyond agenda, in the silence that coexists behind and within all sound.

Simply attending in the stillness of silence can be enough to support a person through a process and to signal the vast space in which they exist beyond their thinking process and their complex webs of personal identity. Beyond invitation or demand, this position is unconditional, and as such leaves the other with the complete freedom to move according to their individual need.

For many, just this atmosphere of stillness is enough to encourage a calming of the mind and an intuition of the possibility of harmony.

Stillness is healing, as a shift can occur in which we (or they) realize that all we could think, do or say, or all that has been thought or said about us, is not who we ultimately are. It is as if the whole social battlefield is devalued by the sudden, awesome strength of the planet. As such, the opening of the way to the stillness of silence has tremendous value to the whole.

15

Collective Consciousness

"The way to liberation is to recognize that consciousness itself is a unified field of humanity."

When a nation stands together, we see a powerful formation and reformation of group consciousness. As with nations, so it is with religions which also mark out time and create unity through sacred ritual.

We also see the formation of group consciousness within tribes, schools of spirituality, football fans, bridge groups and family units, to name a few. Our leaders know this, and they seek the opportunity to boost national consciousness – through the cultivation of events in time such as the Olympics or a royal wedding. They also use the opportunity of collective consciousness to assert control of the 'masses'.

Collective consciousness is a natural and beautiful movement towards togetherness, yet it excludes a deeper unity as group consciousness is most often dependent on either exclusion, recruitment or both. A unity which is pretends to be absolute, yet which is exclusive or conditional, will always at some stage come into conflict with itself.

The persuasive and seductive power of marketing uses the tools of group consciousness through messages and the establishment of landmarks in time. The more successful the marketing, the stronger the polarizing effect: you either are "lovin'" McDonald's or hating it.

Ironically, the latest marketing campaign of Marlboro cigarettes comes under the banner "Just Be." The messages are seductive precisely because they are intuitively responding to the spiritual yearning within the collective human state.

At its best, group consciousness is a relative, evolving collective identity, enlivened by a contribution of individual qualities from members and held in form by structures that support a shared process of evolution.

Yet because consciousness is so closely linked to power, authority, status and pain-based ego structures, this group consciousness needs to be treated with great care and responsibility. That same collective consciousness can collectively project, exclude, stigmatize and condemn those who are excluded.

It would be good if we could strive for the degree of conscious liberation which means that although we are part of the shared consciousness of our country, culture, family or school, we are nevertheless deeply and individually responsible for its direction – even if this means leaving the field or rejecting ourselves. Competition is a healthy part of evolution, but it needs to be liberated as a developmental playground, held lovingly within the deeper wisdom of heart.

The way to this liberation is to recognize that consciousness itself is a unified field of humanity.

Collective consciousness is nothing more than the sum of its individual parts when they surrender to the whole. Its direction can be greatly determined by the loudest voice and the strongest need. As such, the direction can suddenly become destructive – motivated by a fear of suffering rather than attraction towards a shared positive vision. The more a field of collective consciousness defines itself in competition with others, and the results of that competition become definitive, the more destructive its direction is likely to become.

This is one of the greater challenges faced by world teachers, the challenge to their personal human freedom to live as they need. Because in spreading their message, they create a field of collective consciousness, one over which the wounded aspects of individuals can seek to gain control.

Yet bravely, they continue. Because the will at the basis of humanity to evolve and improve our collective state is a deeper imperative overriding fear of self, be it a small self or collective. Yet the projected form of the group on the teacher is never, never who they really are, or who *we* really are. It is just a relative form that exists to inspire a collective evolution.

It is important to remember that these same challenges face us all when we choose to expand our consciousness; it is just a question of scale. The more our consciousness expands, the more we will be flattered, attacked, hunted and crucified. This is because we begin to emanate a light, and light to some can create jealousy as they still hold the belief that it is limited, graspable, and something which can be possessed.

In the choice to develop consciousness, we make a choice for greater power, an increasing ability to impact our direction, and a deeper responsibility for experience.

We will always share our consciousness with others like an overflowing cup. We anyway live in structures of group consciousness. Yet the stronger we are in individual consciousness, the greater our responsibility, whether it is within a relationship, family or a high-tech industry.

To take responsibility means to be vigilant for the highest interest: to develop an ability to respond and to become responsive to the needs of the now.

To not take responsibility can mean we find an abyss where demons created by jealousy, fear, rage and genocide can reign.

16

Conscious Empowerment

"The mind is born to follow experience as the first dictate."

Consciousness has an incredible ability to create reality and affirm it. As the light source at the centre of thought processes, it invests thoughts with a sense of inherent reality. Rapidly after finding the 'I', we begin to load it with identity. Often, we believe that this identity needs to be defended against the 'other'.

"I am a man/woman" (complete with all the latent connotations or beliefs around gender).

"I am intelligent."

"I am generous."

"I am good person."

"I always tell the truth."

"It will end in tears."

Often such 'hooks' or statements we use to hypnotize ourselves are defensive movements of mind. We experience the energy of destruction, and to repress it, we tell ourselves "I am a good person." We say "No" to a charity asking for money, we feel guilt, and the mind rushes to the rescue with an affirmation "I am always generous but..."

This is partly because the mind is born to follow experience as the first dictate. It is reactive. Of itself, and without the rest of human experience, it would be silent.

Working through the polarity of the mind, consciousness divides our permitted experience to increasingly small portions, until at some stage the mental state becomes such a suffering that we either break loose or break down – either by thought, feeling or deed.

The mind works with the 'either-or'. We are good or bad;

generous or mean; virgin or whore; smart or stupid. Our right to exist at all on the planet can seem to be at stake when such fixed identities are challenged. Left unattended, consciousness chooses rapidly between polarities. It invests personal attributes with such power that when it is questioned, it can seem like an existential threat.

Even in the privacy of one's own head, this is a kind of catastrophe of limitation. Yet when we consider our thought forms as they project towards others, the potentially destructive nature of investing thoughts with consciousness becomes more striking. When we begin to identify the 'you' or 'they' with a sense of eternal, absolute truth, we become controlling, cruel and often inhumane.

In the labelling of others, we suffer as much as the 'outsider'. A great affliction of loneliness is born. We attempt to heal this by defining ourselves and others more – dictating to them how they 'should' be or behave in order to be worthy of us (or to ease our sense of isolation). We demand authority not only over who we are, but also over who they are.

Yet even if others comply with our secret needs, we will not deeply believe or trust the connection, any more than we can believe that our own self-identity ("I am young and beautiful.") is forever. We secretly know it as a lie, and the isolation or loneliness becomes worse than ever.

17

Consciousness and the Fear of Death

"It is worthwhile to attend to the physical fact of mortality and the preciousness of physical life, moment by moment."

As long as we are conscious, we will continue to experience the fear of death. Consciousness itself is extremely unstable. As we have seen, it can multitask, create and destroy at will. It can choose to include, dictate the truth, and it can also discard what it wants to reject from the realm of experience. Each night, consciousness blacks out and is surrendered to the layers of deep sleep, or to states of dreaming where its repressive abilities are weakened.

Consciousness is the master of investing form, illusion and projection with life. By hooking into the physical, emotional, and mental forms, it gives them power. Yet that same ability to empower also brings the shadow of disempowerment or death. The creation of illusion betrays its illusory nature.

As such, physical death, beyond the passing suffering and physical pain of the experience, is the key challenge of consciousness. It is not the moment that it slips into the darkness which brings the fear, but the proof of its own ultimate impotence – that all its hooks, investments, creations and structures are forever. They are ultimately unsustainable.

The more consciousness is able to allow the truth of its own relative perspective and the impermanence of all its states and creations, the more consciousness is liberated to be of service to existence itself.

When the conscious will is dedicated to service, the fear of individual death is released. Fear will emerge during the actual death process, but within the art of living, fear becomes an ally which whistles to us: "Wake up and attend, be curious, there is change, something new is emerging." Our full attendance dissolves fear.

In this, it is worthwhile to attend to the physical fact of mortality and the preciousness of our physical life, moment by moment.

18

Consciousness in Trilogy

In any opening of the portal of consciousness, the other windows – awareness and emptiness – will become activated. It is a system. Consciousness is so potent in itself that it will release its vitality through the unified system of a human being.

Awareness will soften, expand and check the experience from a dimension outside of physical time. It will also support the integration of consciousness into the physical.

Emptiness will allow it to quicken and pass, creating the spatial freedom for an intensification of light frequency, through increasing degrees of allowance.

19

The Witness

"The Witness that asks 'Who am I?' is the universal centre of inquiry that leads to processes of cognition which are of service to the whole."

Who am I?

Who is the "I" that is asking? How can we perceive it when it is in itself the starting point of perception?

It is a question that has birthed mystical schools from East to West and in which the answer is most often embedded in the one asking. This is because the answer is formless, beyond words, even beyond human thought. It is the last witness – the particle of individual perception that witnesses thought, physical existence, emotion, birth, death, love, peace, unity and suffering beyond belief.

All that it witnesses does not define it. Yet it is alive, more potent and unconditional than anything we have ever seen or could ever see.

The witness is that which is now witnessing you the reader, as you read these words, at the same time as witnessing your physical position, identity, reactions, body temperature, mood, time of day. It could even be witnessing your awareness spreading out like a protective sensor around your family, or your consciousness of another person in the house and the sounds that they make. It also witnesses your choice to read this book.

The Witness that asks "Who am I?" is the universal centre of inquiry that leads to processes of cognition which are of service to the whole.

It celebrates every understanding, and uses it to ask the next question. It is at the root of inquiry into experience in the present moment (including real time projections or beliefs about the past and future). It seems to have a great hunger for knowledge. Beyond anything we can learn from books or teachers, this is the deeper knowledge – the sense of 'knowing' when the mind finds pure affinity with its object and attains a relative sense of truth.

Around or within the Witness is a clean curiosity. It also seems to be unconditionally attracted to the brightest lights of experience – be they composed of agony or ecstasy, or a synergy of both. When the Witness gets bored, those parts of our thought patterns will lose their form, having exhausted their temporal life. This is one reason why boredom can sometimes be a good thing! Something new is about to emerge.

The Witness does not need to identify itself with thought or form. Indeed, it cannot. It is not that.

It is that part of you which can witness even the process of identification – and liberation from the same form when it is no longer useful. It witnesses it all with the same neutrality.

The Witness is the seed of the portal of consciousness – yet it is not consciousness – which as a means of perception can create or destroy whole worlds. Unmastered, consciousness can even create one or several false witnesses – a controlling, censoring eye – that attempt to edit experience. These false witnesses can also be witnessed and fall away, often with quite a feeling of relief as false witnesses tend to confine experience in a manner that generates suffering.

The Witness is itself always observed by an all-encompassing awareness. Both the witness and the observer of awareness find unity beyond polarity in the pure potency of existence itself.

20

When Witnesses Meet

"Most of us are still too fearful in our physical existence to be able to contain the intensity of the conscious connection."

When one person looks deeply into the eyes of the other, there is a meeting of witnesses. For a timeless moment, we witness each other alive in all of this. This can create such an intensification of energy that the charge of consciousness releases into an awareness of separation, or a wider plane of observation through awareness. The heart opens to take in the separate experience of the other, with a kind of respect born of an unconditional recognition of life.

Yet the two witnesses seem to be separated by eyeballs, brains, bodies, minds, memories, understandings, beliefs and experience. When we witness one another, we also become more aware of the rifts between us, which exist within the whole shared experience. And we return to playing out the great drama of individuality within unity.

It is striking how hard it is for us to stay in connection with each other – witness to witness. We can become ashamed or fearful. Sometimes we use sexuality to release the tension or excitement of life witnessing itself. Often, a moment of connection is enough to install fundamental recognition and respect of life in the other. Most of us are still too fearful in our physical existence to be able to contain the intensity of the conscious connection – the wider show must go on. Yet truly being 'seen', even by a stranger in the street, even for a moment, can turn a ship of suffering around within an individual and signify the way back to life. "I have been witnessed. There is someone out there."

We can connect to others directly from the Witness. In normal circumstances (if we care enough), we take a step back from our own thoughts as all-powerful and give the other their own life or their own Witness.

In this, the communication of different perspectives is made possible and a bridge is built. Although two individuals might never agree or be the same on the level of thoughts, understanding or experience, a sharing of consciousness is made possible by the bridge – which makes individual perspective or the conflict between 'truths' less destructive.

21

The Witness and Prayer

"This is a critical ferry between our individual physical body, our energetic being and our soul."

The Witness wants to know what is going on. It wants to experience and gather information. This would seem to suggest it is also feeding this information to another dimension, backstage from the human drama.

As such, the Witness seems to be able to blow a whistle to universal resources of love, peace and unity, signalling a need to open inner doors to universal support.

This emerges through what we experience as moments of grace through unexpected inflows of love, peace or unity. Such inflows of soulful energy are particularly striking around childbirth and the processes of dying and grief.

The Witness also appears to be a messenger – relaying questions from an individual seeker to a higher source of intelligence and returning with answers, or directions towards the experience needed to come to greater understanding or to come more deeply to life.

As such, the Witness would seem to be a mobile, divisible, expandable personal particle of divine intelligence on the vehicle of consciousness. It is a critical ferry between our individual physical body, our energetic being and our soul, which unconditionally offers the aspects of love, peace and unity. The responsibility for becoming conscious and witnessing the power of our individual consciousness is awesome. It can be a matter of life and death, genocide, dehumanization, or the manifestation of the wisdom of unity through world cooperation for the sake of the whole.

Ironically, the more we are able to invest in the purity of consciousness unhooked from thoughts, the more we gain freedom and flexibility of mind and the more intelligent we can become.

As we begin cultivating the ability to free ourselves and the false witnesses of over-identification with thinking and the contents of thought, we develop a capacity to transcend and to catch an intelligent overview of any experience in time and space.

We also open our access to existence in stillness, where thoughts and projections no longer determine us with the limitations of form.

22

Peace

"The secret agenda of every war is peace."

Beyond the stillness of silence, consciousness is associated with the opening of the portal to the soul aspect of peace. This kind of peace is neither inner nor outer. It is a rich, abundant and highly unconditional presence of peacefulness which descends from above, and can meet itself with a similar ascension from the earth.

Peace exists independently of all polarity and all choices. Without peace, no choice would be possible.

The experience of opening towards universal peace through the development of consciousness is a gift to humanity and the planet. The more we are able to allow peace to move into our energetic system, the more we are able to share it with others and with reactive situations of conflict, cruelty and violence. Our ability to allow peace is connected to how far we have released the idea that we are inherently separate from everything else.

Peace will always appear with aspects of love and unity. Through the opening of the portal of peace through the initiation of consciousness, peace can be experienced in its existential depth with a flavour of objectivity (as if it were coming from outside of ourselves), which brings with it a sense of far greater truth than all our daily activities or even our internal process.

Yet we cannot possess it. It is not possible to possess what we truly are. We can only remove the obscuration and as such become a channel of peace into daily life.

23

Consciousness Now

Right now, you can move into a heightened consciousness. Notice your eyes and the feeling of your eyes as you read this page, attending to the eyes and the witness behind the eyes reading the words.

Notice the sound of the words inside your head as you read. Notice the tone of the voice inside your head as you read the words.

Change the tone of the voice to the opposite gender. Notice the new tone of voice inside your head as you read these words. While noticing the internal voice reading these words, including any side comments or thoughts you might add, begin to attend also to your body.

Connect to your hands: left hand, right hand. Connect to the feeling in the palms of your hands. Connect to the feeling in the tips of your fingers.

Connect to your arms: left arm, right arm. Now, attend to the place where your feet meet the ground: left foot, right foot. Notice the weight of your body.

Notice your attitude to your body.

Notice the sense of how it feels to be in this heavy body, pulled to the earth by gravity, as you are reading these words at this moment. Relax into that.

Take a moment to look up from the page and look around the room, noticing the light, shade, and colour. Notice that you are seeing what you see from a unique perspective. Notice that you control what you choose to see.

Now notice yourself noticing. Look at the witness which is witnessing. Who are you? Who is the one that is witnessing?

Connect again with the body. Connect again with the voice in the head as you read the words on this page.

Close your eyes and witness the space between any words or added thoughts as they arise. Notice how it is to be without thought in this moment.

Relax into the sense of being centred in the centre of your head and allow yourself to witness your existence at this moment, in this body, in this space, on this ground, under this sky. Allow it.

III

Awareness

"A measure of water, when poured into the ocean,
becomes the ocean."

I

The Art of Feeling

"Awareness exposes and arouses our blocked energy into movement and reintegration."

Mystery and depth begins with the 'am'. It is as if the 'I' of consciousness seeks substance to its process of identification. The uncomfortable intimacy of 'I fear' is elaborated into 'I am afraid'. Consciousness reflects on a state of being, but does not fully take it into the world of identity.

The 'am', unhooked of definition, introduces the realm of awareness and being. How does it feel to just 'be', from an essential space of feeling which is not defined by any one feeling or emotion?

Everything we think, feel or experience – everything that comes into our experience from heaven, earth or the depth of the physical body – this is not who we are. We are something far more precious, exquisitely beautiful and miraculous than that. We are the being which contains all form, and exists beyond form.

Awareness is the means of perception which reveals the alchemy of transformation – by allowing hidden or buried aspects of our human experience to come to life. Awareness exposes and arouses our blocked energy into movement and reintegration.

Emanating from the centre of the chest, it can also be called 'felt sense' or sentience. Before the mind gets involved, and even behind the chattering of the mind and the wondering of our consciousness, awareness is in movement in the realm of experience – of feeling and sensitivity.

Before we name a feeling or emotion, or begin to make sense of it, awareness has an opportunity to explore in the realm of living experience. When awareness is strong, we can recognize that 'grief' can feel like 'fear', or that 'fear' is sometimes a kind of excitement or anticipation.

Awareness moves through feeling, before ideas or beliefs are formed. The feelings, instincts and emotions emerging in the dimension of awareness precede and outlive the attempts of the mind to make order.

Our peace of mind will not last if our anger or fear goes unattended. Our stillness beyond consciousness will not be sustained if our experience of loneliness is not addressed through sentient exploration. As such, awareness is central to our coming to life in human form.

2

I Am That I Am

Awareness can also refine as awareness of awareness (as long as consciousness agrees to take a lesser role). As such, an ever-refining inner movement can occur in which the veil increasingly thins between the pure life which we are, and the pure life found within every form. The awareness of awareness can also lead us to the unconditional dimensions of unconditional love and nurture.

Awareness is a strong agent for healing. It could seem a paradox that in order to free ourselves of blocks created by anger, or fear, we need to allow these horrors into our awareness. How could freedom from the monster involve opening the cage? Yet this is precisely the path towards liberation.

When we give repressed aspects of experience the fullest right to exist, we create a space in which we are able to perceive them. Awareness floods through this space, and the rejected feelings or emotions begin to take form – either in the presence of atmosphere or even in shape.

Through becoming aware of these forms, we also notice that our awareness itself, the observer, is more real than that which is observed, no matter how frightening it might appear to be.

The refined feeling attendance of awareness invites the experience to life – to begin to transform. This transformation involves the shedding of layers of experience which are no longer applicable to the living state. This allows the reintegration of the vital energy from which the block was formed. Through the loving and accepting grace of our awareness, blockages become responsive. They begin to move and unpeel. Sometimes it takes moments and sometimes longer. But through this transformation, energy is released by degrees to be reunited within the whole. Through disintegration, reintegration is made possible. As such energetic blocks begin to dissolve; more vitality is available to move through our bodies, hearts and minds, and we become increasingly alive.

Freedom in this context does not mean that negativity and suffering is gone forever. It simply means that we no longer find our sense of self in these states. They do not define who we are.

I am angry, very angry. "I am" is the traveller. The anger is the experience – as fleeting and temporary as steam from a kettle. I am existence experiencing anger. Existence composed of a unique recipe of love, peace and unity. Also, this body is breathing calmly in, and out. The anger can do its thing, without becoming absolute.

"I am that I am" is often represented as the name of God as spoken to Moses when he questioned the identity of the one behind the miracle of the burning bush. Although beautiful in its affinity with the I AM schools of Eastern mysticism, there is a mistranslation here of the original Hebrew. The biblical words with which God is said to answer are: אֶהְיֶה אֲשֶׁר אהיה (pronounced: *Ahiyeh asher ahiyeh*. Literally this means: "be that is being" – a perpetual pulsation of present-tense (or 'tense-less') being.

3

The Healing in Suffering

**"The words 'I am here for you' become a gift that unites
heaven and earth, and one human with another."**

A popular motivation for inner growth is to liberate ourselves
from these unpalatable aspects of human life. We operate with an
unproven belief that there should be no suffering on earth.

In our preciousness, we get entangled again and again in our
escape plans, not understanding that the suffering will continue,
and that the deepest freedom occurs when we can be in the pain
while truly realizing that we are not the pain, but that which is
able to perceive and experience. In this space, it is possible to
channel peace, love and softness into the areas where suffering
prevails.

When we are able to allow the experience of suffering within
ourselves, then the door to compassion is opened. The words "I
am here for you" become a gift that unites heaven and earth, and
one human with another.

The agenda to navigate ourselves away from suffering often
leads us to become entangled in illusion through denial,
repression, or projection of those unwanted sensations on others,
claiming that the source of pain is outside ourselves.

As such, spirituality can become abused as a means to escape
the very energies that most need to be processed – those experiences which are our direct progeny, the demons in our inner
home. Not the demons of the neighbour.

Through inner growth, we do not negate suffering, but we
can perceive it so openly and lovingly that we are able to know
from a fearless space that we are that indestructible source
behind perception. We might be in suffering, but we are not the

suffering. As well as residing in pain, we do not have to also lose our existence, and our peace, love, and togetherness.

As we deepen our connection to existence through opening sentience and the window of awareness, emotional pain and feelings of suffering become more pure, short lived and natural.

They are alive and move through us in the here and now, according to our need to be responsive. The energetic imprint of them is what forms our humanity: our intuition of beauty and our capacity for compassion.

Emotion or feeling no longer needs to fixate through independent form shaped or frozen in time through the dictates of a fear-based mind – which aims to block living experience in its fearsome potency.

4

Feeling the Feeling

"Awareness precedes and underlies consciousness, and the awakening into the physical body."

While consciousness is often described through the metaphor of light, not least because it is so traditionally associated with awakening, awareness is in the first instance more connected with experience, or feeling. Awareness is all about our ability to feel, feelings that often happen in the infinite comfort of darkness.

As such, awareness expands during meditation, when the eyes are closed, in sleep, and in the darkness of not knowing. Our awareness exists beyond thought and can be independent of thought processes. It can even sense the unique atmosphere around ongoing thought processes. Awareness precedes and underlies consciousness, and the awakening into the physical body.

There is a vast difference between the conscious observation of an event, and the awareness of it. Awareness, unlike consciousness, continues through the metaphorical darkness. Far more subtle and less determined by the first appearance of form, awareness opens a new field – that of 'felt sense'. When the Tibetans talk about sentient beings, they are addressing the dimension of awareness. Sentience is common to most forms of life on the planet. Next time you see an animal, connect from the heart. A shared awareness will emerge between you. This is born of sentience and composed of particles of love as existence recognizes itself through the dimension of the heart.

Whereas consciousness will focus light on phenomenon, affirming form, awareness senses, experiences and blends with it.

Awareness means that in perceiving an object (a lady), you attune to far more than her appearance, the words she says, how she moves or what she does. Awareness comes into play when you sense her anger. It is active when you feel a latent fear or need for loving kindness, such that you are unsure if it is yours or hers.

Your awareness is of service to the development of consciousness in revealing too that the word 'woman' evokes a different atmosphere or experience than the word 'lady'. As such, awareness brings the sentient information that gives a heart or feeling to words – and to the thoughts of our mind. Without awareness, we would look like soul-less nerds, or computers. The subtlety of how one word can mean entirely different things according to the feeling investment, atmosphere or tone would be missed.

Did you ever hear "I love you" spoken in a way that the message is clearly "get out of my way"? This is the energetic substance of thoughts, words and form which awareness can perceive.

5

To Be Able to Be

"Awareness doesn't need to know. Rather, it seeks to experience."

Through the development of awareness, layer after layer of experience can be unpeeled (often one layer hooked behind another) until we come to an expansion of our individual Being.

A great expanse of awareness can occur with the experience of falling deeply in love. Awareness itself can spread love just through becoming aware of others.

Each time we say: "I don't know", awareness is given its opportunity. Within the "I don't know", or the surrender of conscious attachment to thought or fact, there is the wonder of not knowing, which is the field through which awareness thrives. Awareness doesn't need to know. Rather, it seeks to experience.

The moment consciousness is awakened into the living miracle of the present moment and you glimpse the potency of existence beyond the temporal frameworks of the linear mind, a new journey is beginning – a journey through awareness to the depths of your being.

Less caught in a need to fixate reality, awareness can move in a refining process through all levels of experience. With the mind silent and in the background, and with consciousness unhooked to a silent witness, awareness is able to allow feelings and states which can open a deeper understanding.

Present beyond cognitive time, awareness continues regardless of past, present and future. It is rather connected to another level of time, which we call sentient time. This is the time it takes for the anger to burn out, or for the grief to transform to love.

Awareness continues during much of sleep, bringing forward dreams which can be scattered fragments of experience that have been rejected by consciousness.

Awareness does not need to focus on a particular object. It can sense the atmosphere of a whole room, city or country. Working from beyond language, it can recognize the collective energy of a particular family. It can expand across the planet, to the heavens and into the heart of the earth, all at once.

You can be aware of the anger of another person, even if you have not physically seen them for months. Awareness is infinite, expandable and able to blend with phenomena. It can perceive independently of time and space.

6

Awareness and Merging

"The opening of the thoughtless window of awareness tends to bring a movement into greater sanity and maturity."

The blend of awareness between people occurs long before a similar unity can be reached in consciousness, and consciousness is the first to reinstate individuality.

Awareness is the field of perception which means you can experience yourself as intensely individual at the same time as part of a living, interdependent whole. It is the field that allows a movement beyond polarity, dualism or 'either-or thinking', and into the 'and-and' possibility of experience. "We are one but we're not the same." I am you and you are me.

As such, the development of awareness creates a need for us to release some of our fears around insanity.

In practice, in a world so focussed on the either-or dualistic thinking of the programmed mind the opening of the thoughtless window of awareness tends to bring a movement into greater sanity and maturity.

Within awareness, different feelings and emotions can exist at the same time. There is space for the manifold expressions of form, without any threat to the unity of creation. There is the openness for many truths and many perspectives – all of which enrich the collective, shared atmosphere or the manifest.

Between people, there is the love of each individual, and the shared love of the whole which is a unique creation and a result of the merging power of awareness. Loyalty to this shared love is the foundation of fulfilling relationships.

7

Between Head and Heart

"In the dimension of awareness, alone could be purposefully misspelt as: all-one."

Awareness is not the same as consciousness, although often awakened experience involves a blend of the two.

Awareness is present in many degrees of sleep. It is often awareness that we use when doing inner exercises with energy or meditation. We are aware of our bodies, even when we are not fully conscious of them. While consciousness touches areas of pain and the skin surfaces, awareness can sense dysfunction in the depths of the body and in areas where there is stress or a physical impact of emotional pain. As such awareness crosses the physical/psychological divide in the emergence of physical disorder or psychosomatic afflictions.

It is also the central place of integration between the non-physical and the physical, and between our separate existence and communion with others.

We are aware from the extrasensory faculty of awareness of the presence of loved ones near and far. We are aware of atmospheres, vibrations and moods – and as such, awareness can move far beyond mind as a source of information. As such, awareness is softer, but far more expandable on the level of humanity than consciousness.

Your awareness can be developed, refined and broadened. It is an area where increasing mastery has a direct equation with long-term self-development or inner evolution, with the opening of the heart and enlightenment.

The development of awareness brings a refinement of feeling and with this an increased ability to manifest our unique qualities into the world.

Consciousness can be used by some as a method to short circuit emotional pain or the grief of the heart. It can create 'spiritual' or 'disentangled' personalities who lack empathy. Unfortunately, this disentanglement can come at a cost of rejection – as parts of experience deemed undesirable are thrown into the emptiness as if they would cease to exist there.

Yet these phenomena have an energetic life born from the life we are. They will haunt us. We can run but we cannot hide. Soon enough they will surface through the felt sense of awareness, bringing an opportunity for healing.

This is not written from a place of judgement. Sometimes, short-term survival gives us no option but to temporarily discard parts of our experience. But who will remind us to regather the pieces when the battle is over? We will always have cause to remember.

Awareness is inclusive, permissive and compassionate. It is also indispensable to inner work which involves allowing and inviting the deeper degrees of suffering into the original light.

For some time, we can use consciousness to repress unwanted emotion, or unwanted manifestations in the outer or inner world. We can even use our consciousness to attempt to block our awareness. But the awareness will stay anyway, to tell its story through dreams or through the places we find ourselves attracted to or repelled from, or through the ways we act out in the world.

Consciousness can direct awareness, but it is awareness that will invite the deeper revelations, which can then be allowed by consciousness and opened in a process of relative cognition through an understanding and respect of feeling.

We have less control over our awareness than over consciousness, although in our wisdom, we can employ our consciousness to direct our awareness for our highest interests. We can also join up with a wise friend or teacher to serve us in this process.

Awareness can lead us to consciously or even unconsciously take responsibility for the way we respond in any given moment. Ingrained in the word responsibility is the ability to respond. This responsiveness is a direct function of our capacity to allow all aspects of experience into the light. Responsiveness occurs in awareness whether or not consciousness allows it. That is, whether or not we want it, we are responding anyway. If someone in the room hates you, you are responding from the dimension of awareness, even if your consciousness plans to ignore it.

Awareness opens our freedom by giving permission to all aspects of ourselves to exist: whether beautiful, sour or antisocial. And when we allow these aspects to exist, the more we allow the promise of integration and healing.

A development of awareness can lead us to experience our own separation and loneliness and yet to be aware of others in the same chamber of isolation and despair. Through awareness, we are less alone. In this sense, alone could be purposefully misspelt as: all-one.

Awareness is an expression of being which allows many truths to exist at the same time, and for everything in the universe to have its place, softly allowing phenomena into consciousness.

During energy exercises, awareness is a key tool. During meditation, consciousness can suddenly become unconsciousness or a drop into sleep when you meet a habitual block in your inner world. It could be that you previously learned that if consciousness pushes with effort against an energetic block, then its effect can be to make the block more rigid or to stir up anger, fear or rejection. So the mind does its great all-or-nothing movement and surrenders to the known space of sleep. This can be good; as in sleep, awareness can move with more freedom. But it also signals a need to move more deeply with sentience and careful attention to the realm of feelings and felt experience.

Awareness allows the block to exist; it has no agenda and is not at war. Awareness can fuse unconditionally with phenomenon within yourself and others, creating a permission which allows the unfolding of a story. Alternatively and at the same time, awareness can reside around a block, for as long as necessary, until movement begins of its own accord.

8

Love

"Even the agony of grief is made of particles of frozen love awaiting liberation."

Perception through awareness is so closely associated with the feeling of love, that some teachers have stated that awareness itself is love. Certainly, those masters who open the windows of awareness and lead their followers to an experience of being are the recipients of waves of loving gratitude, bordering on attachment. This is needed, as a field is created around the master or teacher which serves the whole.

Anchored energetically in the centre of the Heart chakra, which is the area covering not only the physical heart but the whole central area, awareness in its natural movement is indeed a channel of the feeling of love between people, and between an individual and creation. When the channel is open, life falls in love with itself again and again, and the mission to dissolve any form blocking that path becomes a mission empowered by love for all that is.

However, the perceptive faculty of awareness is itself neutral. Awareness can be a vehicle that communicates our state to others. It can also transmit an atmosphere of fear, stress or passive anger, for example. This is how others can sometimes sense beyond our nervous smile, for example, and pick up our hidden afflictions such as despair, insecurity, or jealousy.

The more we navigate our way through the layers of feeling in the area of the heart, the more we are able to open its doors to allow the movement of this universal love through awareness outwards.

It is important to note that the love is 'allowed' by us to be carried on awareness or welcomed by awareness. It occurs naturally when we stop interfering and surrender.

Love is the aspect of universal soul which is directly accessible through the deployment of awareness. As such it is abundant, unconditional and deeply healing. The limitations to the amount we are suffused with the unconditional love are set only by our fears, our self-rejection, or natural, physical limitations.

There is as much love available to us in any given moment as we are prepared to allow. Love is a key component in holding creation in unity – creation which involves the temporary division of life into a multitude of forms.

Just as the peace which is the backdrop to consciousness can be unveiled unconditionally through clearing consciousness of its hooks in the thoughts of the mind, so can the clearance of energetic hooks open the way for unconditional Love which is the universal backdrop to awareness.

Each soul aspect will often bring with it a sense of the other. As such, a deep, all-pervasive experience of Love will often bring with it overtones of peace and unity.

These soul aspects are unlimited and unconditional – the part of the creator which resides in us and which we can invite into our lives as we manifest ourselves on a daily basis. They can support and nurture. They are suffused with grace and mercy.

We are surprised by them sometimes as if they were visitors from another world at key moments in our lives. But actually, they are not visitors; we are simply liberating our existence through the release of the limitations of our beliefs.

Yet although the soul is our anchor, container and unconditional support to human living, and although its appearance through the cracks of experience leaves a benchmark of guidance for future orientation, in itself it is not enough for healing.

Complete healing requires a deeper development of the three windows of perception – through which we are interacting as human beings.

9

Enlightenment and Sexual Polarity

"Our sexuality is a powerful ally, containing a circulation of the purity of both male and female aspects."

A central concern of many is around the area of intimacy and personal relationships. This is the front line on the horizontal plane; where we perceive one another beyond habitual patterns and the deeper layers of emotion and feeling emerge.

Our deeper wounds tend to play out in our intimate relationships and this seems to be the basis of many contracts of real life learning and self-development.

A key characteristic of the central dimension of the heart is the movement beyond polarity, from the 'either-or' to the 'and-and'. In this, intimate relationships challenge the opening of awareness and the opening of the heart, for it is here that we truly move towards wholeness in connection with another.

In the interaction between people there is a physical manifestation of the active-receptive and still dynamic present within each moment of physical life. It is in finding the stillness behind polarity, and the freedom to move authentically and naturally through action and reception, that we uncover the beauty of movement through life and manifestation.

A key part of this opening is expressed by gender separation. Many couples, not only heterosexual, are engaged in a shared process in which compatibility allows the development and realization of complimentary aspects.

In moving beyond polarity with a partner, we begin to uncover and allow the opposite polarity within our experience. To realize the extreme of the feminine side of ourselves naturally beckons the male aspect. To move deeply into the male aspect, we evoke the female. This is a perpetual dance within each of us, and through the blend of male and female we are able to move beyond polarity together and to open the sources of unconditional love.

This can mean an active inquiry into uncovering an awareness of the inner male and the inner female. Through the invitation of the male and female to come into blend, a deeper love is allowed – one that moves from behind and before this first polarity in creation. Sometimes this experience is projected psychically outwards on another of the opposite sex, often one who represents complete openness of heart and allowance such as Jesus. Leading to the deeper opening of the heart and the rising of kundalini energy, this process is commonly known as enlightenment.

In this, our sexuality is a powerful ally, containing a circulation of the purity of both male and female aspects.

In its unhealed state, however, sexuality can reflect the whole dynamic of imbalance between consciousness, awareness and emptiness, and between manifestation and surrender.

In the process of opening our awareness, it is important to maintain a vigilance of where we are putting conditions on love as a result of our wounded attitudes towards gender – either the attitude of our male aspect towards our inner female or vice versa.

The beliefs embedded around the gender split are the fences we must pass to return to the Eden of the heart, and which we must negotiate to keep the way to Eden open in our daily life and personal relationships.

Part of this involves a permission to experience also the painful feelings of rejection, betrayal, shame or abandonment as nothing more or less than feeling itself – breathing through the experience and staying present to the felt sensation. In sentient time, some basic attitudes to the male or female 'other' can be healed through the strong wind of unconditional love which in itself wishes for nothing except the well-being of existence in physical form.

10

Active: Healing

"A feeling does not need to be explained or understood in order to be alive and lived out in its evolving totality."

Everything alive has an element of push, pull and still; active, receptive and perceptive.

In its active form, awareness can move into form, become the form and expand beyond the form. It can blend with the other, without the need to change or fix anything. Awareness can timelessly access atmospheres on the other side of the planet or even in distant galaxies. Unhooked from form, your awareness is able to fill the universe. It can become one with the awareness of God, or with its own infinite universal source.

Awareness can be an active vehicle for consciousness when we seek to consciously replace ourselves in the experience of another. It is a vital ingredient of empathy.

The more we are able to master our awareness through expansion into experience and the refinement of experience (through focussing awareness), the more we know that that which we experience is not that which we truly are. We are not that. We are the one experiencing it, in all its transient subtleties.

When used actively, awareness can be directed by consciousness, the Witness or by universal need. You can bring your awareness to the area of suffering in a friend and your awareness will merge with the other, activating a process of acceptance, integration and realization.

In moving outwards towards aspects of you or of another, an attitude of softness and loving kindness is a tremendous support. The softness of our awareness means we reach out in a way which is sprinkled with receptivity – meaning we are more precisely attuned to the need of the moment within the form that we are moving into. Softness allows the caress of perception, and it allows us to perceive with more refinement.

This is a treasure house of qualities which in an exquisite synergy expresses the pure individuality of what we individually have at this moment to express in the world. This essence can be experienced through moving to the physical area with awareness and 'being' there, allowing it to unfold in a gentle and undisturbed manner. It can also be activated by positioning consciousness in this position.

This evolving formation of qualities or talents is specific to this lifetime, or to this period of time. It is an exquisite composition of the living aspects of you in creation right now, drawing in both the eternal and the genetically possible at any given moment. To experience this essence is at first similar to blending with an all-powerful sun.

The more we are able to stay in essential being, the more there is a loosening of the area, allowing manifestation of qualities and also increasing accessibility to qualities not normally seen as 'ours'.

Charged with the love of the heart dimension and exuding the atmosphere of your unique presence, this essence of you is what you are here to express. It is an individually transient configuration from a universal well of infinite qualities.

Like a sun, it blazes outwards as a gift towards humanity and to creativity itself. The more the Witness is able to reside within this core of essential being, the more it too evolves.

In a way, this essential core is the powerful fire of purpose which is part of the reason for our personal incarnation. It brings with it a deep human responsibility to be of service.

It is clear that releasing consciousness from identification with thought patterns and emotional form is a critical part of awakening and reawakening at every opportunity in the process of living.

The movement involved here is an unhooking of our conscious identifications through the use of a latent wisdom of emptiness. In this movement of unhooking, a space is created through which there is an infusion of awareness through the heart dimension.

Perception through awareness occurs at the heart of a polarity between consciousness and emptiness. As such, the faculty of awareness is extremely important in the process of integrating spirituality with the physical, and the physical experience with the spiritual.

Awareness is also the sentient faculty which moves through the horizontal plane, connecting us as individuals with the world outside, and with others.

Even more importantly, awareness is the means through which we can experience beyond the level of mind and thought processes. For example, we can experience a physical pain, or a sudden flash of emotion, and the experience does not need to be named, explained or understood in order to be alive and lived out in its evolving totality.

Through awareness, we can blend with what at first feels like a physical pain in an organ. As we allow the experience of pain into awareness, we can begin to experience its refinement. It can have sharp edges, it can be bitterer in some patches than others. Sometimes, we will become distracted by another pain in the body. We move there. Looking back, we could observe that the pain has actually shifted its position. It is not dominantly physical! It is on the move!

Most of the time, at some stage, a layer of emotion will emerge. Habitually, the thinking mind will use the sword of consciousness to cut a division between the pain in our body and our emotion. In this way, it allocates a certain form and both are temporarily contained (they will not interfere too much with its freedom to talk to itself).

When we move with awareness and with feeling, then the

feeling itself can be invited to refinement. Let us say we experience a feeling we have named anger. Whereas before it was a red flag on the floor, as it merges with awareness it becomes an old carpet. As you hover closer, you can begin to experience that it has depth, softness, and an intricate pattern.

Also, as your awareness blends with emotion, you can begin to notice the age of the emotion. Has it been there forever – perhaps since childhood or earlier? Is it a new arrival, still smelling of its originating factory? Does it have the sense of something which has grown boring, no longer bringing either a learning or protection in its presence? We could even be curious to take a look at what is beneath the carpet. It is in our house, after all.

As emotion or feeling takes form, it is seen with clarity. We are not the feeling, but the awareness which is able to experience it. We are not the awareness, which itself can refine, but something behind that. The transient emotion of anger can no longer define who we are.

11

Receptive: Acceptance

**"In being, we give ourselves the unconditional right to exist
as responsive, sentient existence in physical form."**

Just as awareness can expand outward, it is also a tremendous
receiver. As it is of itself universal, we are able to receive far more
into our awareness than we are prepared to believe.

Not all of this is expected. It is an area where we have far less
control than in the domain of perception through consciousness.
For example, we can start our day in a great state of happiness,
opening our awareness and sending happiness vibes throughout
energetic network with which we are connected with the
universe. By the afternoon, we can suddenly find our state
broken. There is the emergence of a sense of uneasiness, apprehension or fear. This could be an aspect of our inner-process
which can come forward precisely because of the expansion of
awareness. It could also be that there is about to be a terror attack
in the country. At some stage we will understand the experience,
but not in the first instance.

The moment we try to 'know' what is going on, our experience
is blocked. In this, the degree of receptivity in the field of
awareness is closed down. We experience less, and ironically we
get less information about what is going on.

A quick way to check the balance within ourselves between
active and receptive awareness is to contemplate our feelings
around two aspects of ourselves.

1. How easy is it for us to share love with others?
2. How easy is it for us to let ourselves be loved?

In being, we give ourselves the unconditional right to exist as responsive, sentient existence in physical form. Contact with animals and nature greatly supports 'being' as it is a state which underlies and precedes the distinguishing activities of mind.

Being is a beautiful, responsive and healing dimension from which to perceive the inflow and outflow of energies in the present moment. Its principle is intimately connected with living in the here and now. Whatever you experience, think or feel in this moment, be that. Yet in being that, there is a living suffusion of allowance and love towards whatever is manifest in the moment.

This is possible because at the depth of yourself, you know that whatever you experience, think or feel in this moment, you are ultimately not that.

12

Still: Pure Being

Behind all form, and emerging with the backward movement of refinement of awareness through awareness of awareness, is a universal dimension of pure-being.

Beyond the fear of death and beyond form, and before sentient time and space, this dark and abundant resource offers a spaciousness, peace and love – affirming universal existence and presence from beyond the place of qualities and manifestation.

In this dimension, of pure awareness, even our individual energetic qualities do not define us. They are cosmic jewels we are charged to express – but they are not who we are. As such, this is an eternal, unconditional space of infinite love.

From this position, the body moves, but we clearly do not move. Our voice speaks, but we are not speaking. The world is happening but we are not happening. Attentive and containing, this space is a place of subtle rest and comfort.

This dimension of stillness as an aspect of existence can arise from the ecstasy of physical life as experience in the refining dimension of awareness.

13

Unique Qualities

"Essence is partially blind in that its need, like a sun, is to be allowed to shine."

The more we move into being, the more we allow the loosening of our innate qualities – those gifts such as musical expression, mathematics, tidiness or humour which are available to us to share with the world. You can recognize your individual qualities in the feeling of easiness, freedom and joy which arises through expression.

These essential qualities can be felt behind the sternum, often with a warm charge of passion and love. These are the ingredients of our interaction with the world and of our attraction towards other.

Why can it seem so hard yet so attractive to follow the Nike command: 'Just Do It'?

There are quite a few layers of suffering around essence – reasons for not going there – which obscure our essential being. This can include layers of depression, self-rejection or disgust at cruelty. Precisely these areas of experience are transformative when we invite them into our awareness. We are on the way to our sacred home in the physical dimension.

All those wounds stand in potency at the root of surface manifestations, as reasons to divide our awareness from our essential purpose. They are bound together in form by the excuses we carry for not being who we need to be. Indeed, when consciousness falls short of essence and hooks into mental explanations for these layers of suffering, our prison becomes a moated fortress.

Essence is partially blind in that its need, like a sun, is to be allowed to shine. It shines unconditionally – on the whole show. It is beauty itself, and it opens the doors of perception to beauty in all dimensions. We become aware of a depth of beauty in detail which is deeper than pleasure or pain and in this sense beyond dualism. We become increasingly aware of the inherent beauty of all aspects of our world and within the physics of creation.

In the essential dimension, beauty will always find itself. To be fully alive within essence is to experience ecstasy.

14

Shared Awareness

"Through shared awareness we are able to surrender individuality to togetherness."

Ultimately, all awareness is shared. Just as all consciousness, in the purity of its source, is one.

Because of this, blend is possible. You can blend or merge your awareness with the awareness of a flower. We share awareness often with our colleagues at work and with our families. We even share awareness with our whole community, with our city and with the planet. Can you recall the atmosphere in the world after 9/11? This was global awareness as humanity as a whole experienced a definitive shock and twist in its story. Out of this shared awareness, the individual perspective of consciousness emerges.

People can unconditionally share the depths of themselves through blend or through merging with others. Through shared awareness in the here and now, we are able to uncover layer after layer of false self through a willingness to surrender individuality to togetherness.

In this, awareness is a servant of unity, and to the wisdom of interdependence and inter-being which is of service to the whole. A step beyond the deepest intimacy, awareness offers spaces of unity which can have a positive impression on limiting attitudes of mind and beliefs.

Yet be careful. Unity is a direct function of our ability to also contain the pain of transient separation through form, different perspectives, ideas and beliefs. If we cannot contain the differences and apparent rejection within the manifold, we will not be able to access unity. The more we move into shared awareness, the more defiantly the ego can fight back, seeking to maintain its domination through status, privilege or through jealousy and competition.

In trilogy, consciousness, emptiness and awareness are intensely concentrated in the area of Essence. All three powers of perception work like potions in the unveiling of its presence.

Yet awareness and the attitude of softness are the most helpful tools in this invitation to let essential being shine across all borders. Through the integrative wind of awareness, Love, Being and Essence can become one living gift to the universe.

15

The Observer

"The observer is quite unconditional to whether the feeling is positive or negative, happy of painful. Timelessly present, it observes it all."

Just as we traced our way back to a universal witness of supreme intelligence or divine spirit in the dimension of consciousness, it is also possible to move back through a refinement of awareness to the universal perceptive origin. This we have called the Observer.

There is a significant qualitative difference between the Witness and the Observer. The observer is that which is behind that which is able to feel or experience. When we experience a deep sense of love, or peace, for example, this is also seen – it is observed from a position of containment. Even in a situation of chaos or confusion, the observer is there, containing all feelings, forms and manifestations.

When we move to the dimension of feeling, we can notice that the observer is quite unconditional to whether the feeling is positive or negative, happy or painful. Timelessly present, it observes it all.

The Observer is also beyond space. When we are travelling, it can be observed that the body moves, functions, changes country. But the observer does not move. The person is happening, but the Observer does not 'happen'.

The movement into awareness of awareness and to the universal space of observation requires great softness and allowance.

In a sense, the Witness and consciousness needs to be allowed to dissolve so that it does not interfere. The gentle inquiry into the sense through which we feel and, behind that, towards that which is observing the energetic movement within us is sensitive. As we move into pure awareness, the importance of vibration emerges, and as vibration refines through attendance to the full silence behind vibration, an observer emerges.

This can be rapidly lost, but with cultivation and practice we can open an increasing capacity to reside in a non-dual state of observant awareness. This awareness does not perceive form as solid, but runs through the whole, rejecting nothing. In a way, it is like becoming the sentient heart of God.

Loyalty to the observer, in the sense that rather than tracking experience we attend to that which is able to experience, is worthwhile in that it vastly increases our capacity to allow the manifestation of energetic form – unconditionally to fears based on identity. Nothing is lost in this. We can make all the conscious order and structure from what has been seen later.

We do not need to reach for the observer. It is always there. It emerges when the way is clear – often just before we go to sleep, or minutes prior to awakening to full consciousness.

Sometimes, when we recall a sequence of events, it is possible to also recognize that this too was observed. We were present as the observer even if in that moment we did not recognize it. In truth, we are all always also present as the cosmic observer of all manifestation.

IV

Emptiness

Why Not Be Empty?

"Oh yes, I *know* all about Emptiness."

The 'here' is perhaps the most important part of the trilogy. Through the 'here' all hidden agenda to transcend the burden of human responsibility, or to take flight from the challenge of existing in physical form, is removed. Through the 'here', unhooked of individual physical location, we are able to begin liberation from the limitations of space. Yet 'here' is also specific to the manifestation of existence in physical matter, or life on earth. It denies nothing.

Emptiness is a difficult word. It seems to be hollow, a void, and most of its connotations are negative. There is 'nothing' in it.

Indeed, a good friend suggested I fill this section with 30 blank pages. But then we agreed that this wouldn't work, as there would still be the paper... and the idea created by the gimmick... the smell of the book... perhaps for all that, a page number. Actually, we thought the page numbers in this section could start to move in reverse.

The truth is that for many seekers, emptiness is annoying. It is a Buddhist idea which is abstract, conceptual, and not entirely relevant. It trashes everything.

All true.

It is also a portal of perception, so all-pervasive, apparently unspiritual and yet constantly used that we become increasingly unable to notice how much it is part of every living thought, feeling and object. This resource is alive and it is ours.

Emptiness is an immediate insult to the mind.

Let's think about this later.

First I need to deal with my ____ (fill in the blank).

It's meaningless. (True too, it is really not about meaning.)

I'm not there in my process (what process?).

If I want emptiness, I will go to a Tibetan teacher.

When the potent energy of emptiness is first sensed or apprehended by an awakened consciousness, it can be so outrageous that consciousness shakes itself up even more, checks in on itself, and again asserts itself with full force. The suggestion of emptiness immediately brings consciousness to life.

Protectively, consciousness moves to contain this new entity in the shop of inner growth.

Yes, I know all of this. But you are wrong. Emptiness is not empty. Fact. You are probably talking about Stillness.

Yet everything we witness and experience in heaven, hell and earth is in motion. It was born and it will die. This moment is one of a million dying moments. And this too will pass. All that exists is in movement by virtue of the emptiness between, around, within and beyond these illusions of form. Without emptiness, there is truly no-thing. No form. Everything would collapse into a dense grain. Form depends on it!

Emptiness allows form, it permits expression, and it is the paramount ingredient of structure, of creation. Through emptiness, we expand. Emptiness is simply the perception that that which is seen is empty of a separate self.

Stillness of silence pervades the room. Thought is born.

Yes, there is something, but emptiness is the wrong word for it.

Having claimed the right to name this new beast in paradise, the conscious mind could then be activated by a fear of its own extinction to play out a drama. This time it is a sophisticated, highly-developed enactment of the war between good and evil.

What is this infinite night, this chaos, this dark energy that would annihilate all that I am?

Is this the realm of Satan?

At least, if Satan reigned there, it wouldn't be empty, would it? Somebody has to be in control!

After a while, consciousness relaxes and can forget about this emptiness thing. It's just a 'thing', after all. But it's too late, because the power of awareness – aroused by the recent lightning storm of consciousness – has also begun to stir.

The thoughts above are in shock and fighting to cling on; the fears below are bristling up, getting ready to freeze, fly or fight the disturbance to form.

There is also a deep rage uncurling with a hiss of that most foul word: rejection.

What is this that has so upset the holy head? Is there also a threat to the sacred heart?

Awareness begins to expand outward, in search of this phenomenon (for now) called emptiness.

Perhaps it can be healed?

Yet emptiness can be even more annoying to those that have chosen to dwell through the dimensions of awareness and the human heart. It is important for these people to feel themselves as generous, open and non-rejecting. The heart would sacrifice itself in order not to reject. They tend to be idealists, and therefore cling with a spiritual passion to the illusion of independent self and the integrity of form.

The heart has long opened and reopened itself to love so many times in a worthy movement of vigilance on behalf of the whole. As such, emptiness can seem slightly nasty.

Awareness is highly able to contain the 'and-and'. It can let many truths exist at the same time. This is its beauty. It can surrender itself to grief and it can develop itself through love. A good part of most traumas can be healed through awareness, but the redemption is not really complete without perception through emptiness.

The open heart gives everything in the universe the fullest permission to exist. Except – and here is the irony – that which is the source of rejection. This feared unconditional rejection, through perception through emptiness, seems to invalidate even the states of bliss, ecstasy and stillness which have until now brought so much. These too are relative.

Hesitantly and generously, awareness moves towards this sensation of emptiness like a patient mother towards her needy child. She reaches out to this feeling of emptiness with affirming presence.

"All that there is on heaven and earth is composed of love."

"ONLY NOT!" says the child.

"Love is the ultimate reality behind everything."

"ONLY NOT!"

"Emptiness is just a kind of awareness."

"ONLY NOT!!!"

"Emptiness doesn't exist!"

The two year old leaves the house to go play with the traffic, leaving a great, empty space between them.

In meeting the challenge of emptiness, some will insist with an increasing determination on pure awareness as the absolute self, or on consciousness as the source of life. They have not discovered that, in plunging into emptiness, that which composes every aspect of experience, perception and perspective begins to be liberated: this is existence itself.

2

Self-Realization

"It is now time to move through the relativity of time and space and to remember, allow and cultivate this natural human means of perception."

Awakening at the level of consciousness, and enlightenment at the level of the heart are events which initiate whole new processes of self-discovery. Sometimes these processes can take years to integrate, and sometimes there is a fall back to an old state in which to be enlightened becomes an aspect of personality, an egoic hook, or a memory of an event. To truly move into the manifestation of existence in human form, it is necessary to open the process of self-realization which is made available through perception through emptiness. Paradoxically, in order to be truly of service in the world of form, we need to realize that form is illusory. It is not absolute.

It is now time to move through the relativity of time and space and to remember, allow and cultivate this natural human means of perception.

Although many of us 'know' emptiness conceptually as the latent, inherent space behind all uncreated form as described by Buddhist tradition, few have dared to actively espouse it as *a means of perception* through which we can experience our world.

Yet, the clear sight of emptiness is integral to the way we experience and the way we feel, think, act and communicate. It is at least as important as consciousness and awareness as a source of wisdom in every choice.

It is through the clear sight of emptiness that our deeper karmic states and beliefs are realized and released from existence as non-absolute. The process can be humbling for those of us who believed our work was done, but it is deeply worthwhile in not only opening the other means of perception more widely, but also in releasing fear, unsupportive attitudes and core issues with physical embodiment in human form.

3

Everyday Emptiness

"Emptiness is not nothing; and in emptiness, nothing is lost."

We actually use a latent wisdom of emptiness all the time – every moment we release a thought, an experience or a sound. Physical vibration is experienced through emptiness. How could any aspect of our being be present or manifest without it? How could it find form? How could we create and how could we destroy?

How could we become impregnated with consciousness?

Both consciousness and awareness utterly depend on the real, all-pervasive backdrop of emptiness in order to exist, to focus, to merge with each other and to expand.

Our allowance of emptiness relates directly to our ability to unveil the Witness, our essential being and to become the Observer. It directly impacts our ability to grow and develop, and to move with freedom. It is integral to the expansion of love and the sharing of peace.

Emptiness is not nothing, and in emptiness, nothing is lost.

'Nothing' itself suggests a separation between form and non-form. There is the thing and there is the no-thing. Emptiness sees through and beyond this separation. Form itself is composed of emptiness. It is not separate.

This ubiquitous emptiness, which runs through every particle of who we are, through every thought, feeling, perception, perceptive form or rock and stone, is so familiar to us and so intimately part of our composition that we can fail to notice it is there. Yet when we allow that which is so known, so commonplace, so intimate to truly appear as the inherent truth to all we are and all we will ever be, the sense can be of a surprising homecoming. The absolute was always right here, now, directly under the nose. We are eternally safe. We have come home.

4

I Suffer Therefore I Am

"Suffering does not define who you are."

To begin to experience living through emptiness, especially for the Western mind, is quite explosive. We are ready to accept that the less subtle phenomena – such as our point of view or passing feelings – are illusions, but what about our deepest attitudes, beliefs, fears, and survival strategies?

This takes time, both linear time and sentient time. The burning of illusion or the exposure of core feelings of unworthiness, pain or rage involves patience in which the recruitment of the eternal observer is a tremendous support.

It is burning, but I do not burn. It is suffering, but I do not suffer.

It also takes time for the nervous system to adjust and for our minds to reflect on what is occurring as deeper wisdom emerges.

Ironically, the last illusions to fall are not our greatest joys, but our beliefs in an inseparable attachment between existence and suffering. This is because suffering, beyond all else, requires attachment and is also a result of attachment. The rejection of suffering, or the attempt to avoid it through denial, creates a core entanglement.

Sometimes it seems that we hook ourselves into our suffering as if we believed that if we didn't suffer, we would die. "I am drowning, but as long as I am in pain, I know I will live." When spoken out, it seems like a crazy logic – but it was one of the ways our minds made sense of the challenge of physical incarnation.

The pleasant aspects of being in physical form are taken for granted and unremarkable to our spiritual being – but this suffering – the jab of the needle, the cold hands of the nurse, the shock of breathing and the sudden isolation – this must be an inherent part of human living.

As transient human beings, we have invested in our pain. It makes us feel alive. Imagine a baby experiencing a formless unity within the loving warmth of his mother's arms and with the peaceful, safe presence of his father nearby. Within the warm, supporting atmosphere, the baby is being fed, and sometimes he looks up with his eyes to observe his mother. She is part of him. But then a nurse comes in, lifts up his helpless leg with hygienic fingers, and inserts what is relatively a giant needle into the sole of his tiny foot. The shock and the agony of the traumatic moment engulf perception. He *is* agony. Being physically alive is this agony. At least, this agony is there too. It is the most alive, shocking experience he has had so far as a physical being. It is not out of random sadomasochism that so many mystical traditions use a cultivation of pure agony in order to realize that we are inherently not the pain, but the one which is able to experience pain.

Once we begin perceiving the world through emptiness, the illusions of intransience or the fixed nature of form begin to fall like dominos. One by one or in groups, they are experienced, lived, realized and left behind.

It is in this way that we gain the deeper freedom to re-illusion our world in a way that we choose and which does not ultimately define us. Out of this freedom, that choice will be based on a passion to be of service – according to the simplest and deepest ethics of the heart, and the clearest sanity of mind.

5

Refuge and Sanctuary

"Imagine that in this space, the lack of ground to stand is replaced by an infinite holiness – the sanctity of life itself."

Emptiness is also the space where we discard – with a divisive swipe of consciousness – those aspects of our experience that we do not want to exist. It is the dumping ground of that for which we would disallow or disown, to be rejected from the collective fields of perception.

It is the container of murdered babies, hideous human shame, addicts, family shame and all that is taboo. Great parts of our collective and personal human experience are forsaken in the emptiness by our failure to allow aspects of manifestation.

This cry of the rejected aspects of life is passionately expressed through the powerful, authentic voices of musicians and artists that have realized the vast illusion of collective mind, and regardless of physical survival or social law begin to sing the songs of the perimeters of emptiness.

Yet emptiness is the place we find ourselves, outrageously safe, in the midst of disaster or shock we never imagined we could withstand. It is behind our private escape door – that intimate, cynical, secret zone beyond illusion where we know we are still alive even if the whole world betrays us. It is not a space of suffering. On the contrary, it is a space of tremendous mercy. This is simply because it rejects nothing.

Emptiness is a known space to all of us, in every moment of memory and in experience. It is behind the silence which every composer knows is the definitive tool for the creation of sound. It is in the space between objects and between shadows – that space which allows the greatest refinement and most sacred precision in expression through works of art.

It is active in the breaking of white light into colour, and it is the facilitator of darkness. It is also the space which allows us to experience the atmospheric wordless beauty of a flower, tree or animal, or even the miracle of our own feet, activating our inner world. It is the space between and within each atom, particle and molecule of physical life. It is potent beyond belief.

Emptiness is that which allows us to touch, and to move with the tremendous strength of gentleness in physically contacting our bodies and the bodies of others. It allows us to taste whatever is there in the moment without rejection. It brings this opening of the senses, because in emptiness there is no fear, as in emptiness nothing is lost. As such, perception through emptiness facilitates an unconditional connection and recognition between your existence and all existence.

It is not that which consciousness awakens which is of issue; it is consciousness itself. It is not the glorious and vast expanse of evolving experience in our awareness which is of value, but the refinement of awareness itself. It is not our excellent scientific ability to release all our beliefs, thoughts, feelings and old states which are the miracle; it is the emptiness through which we are able to let go.

Just imagine for a second that this emptiness is suffused with a timeless spirit attuned to who you are, so integral to every molecule of your body and every moment of your experience that you might hardly notice it is there.

Imagine that it is the most familiar, integral source of eternal strength in the universe. That its power sustains, supports and nurtures every moment of manifestation. Imagine that in this space, the lack of ground to stand is replaced by an infinite holiness – the holiness of life itself. This is the kind of atmosphere that suffuses the eternal space of emptiness.

6

Living Through Emptiness

"Through emptiness, we gain the liberation of perspective."

If we softly move with our consciousness to the energetic area around the coccyx or tailbone, we can begin to blend with its feeling. In being there, movement is created.

The coccyx is full of power. At the base of the spine, it is the energetic seat of the sympathetic nervous system. Within this hard case of bone called the coccyx is the energetic point of initiation of perception through emptiness.

When you are ready, allow this presence at the base of yourself to become perception. Open the eyes and ears of the witness at the coccyx and begin to perceive the world from there.

At first, there could be a tremendous relativity in the area of physical sensation. Right now, we see things from this perspective. But there is also another perspective, and another. Perspective is totally relative and is changing all the time. Thought. Sensation, vibration, feeling. Let the mind support the process, but softly keep replacing consciousness into the coccyx.

The eyes can become relativized as vision begins to broaden and awareness begins to flow with strength through the spaciousness. Right now, we hear these sounds in the far distance. But there are also sounds arising in the mid distance, within our bodies, within our imagination. Allow it all. It is all relative. It is not inherently real. It cannot be grasped. It arises and is gone.

Feelings emerge. Perhaps you are walking. There are many sensations at once. The feeling of your feet on the ground, perhaps a pebble for a moment sensed beneath the sole of the shoe. The air on the face. The ache within the physical body. The freedom of movement of the body, which can also be experienced as a passing non-freedom.

It is all inherently empty. It passes more quickly than a thought. It moves through our physical body and experience more rapidly than consciousness can dictate. We can be with the many layers of sensation only through total allowance. Let yourself BE in the coccyx. If there is sadness in your being... Be there with the sadness. If irritation sparkles through, be there in that. Notice that this too will pass, just as you are passing through it. Experience presence in the coccyx, noticing how experience itself comes, goes, and is in constant flux. Here is a deep pain in the dimension of the heart. It was not there before, yet here it is in full feeling. It is not inherently real. Move with your being of emptiness into this pain. Check if you find any space where it can hold you for eternity. Notice that this pain too is inherently empty.

Move with the perception of emptiness to your hands. Experience your hands. You can perhaps feel the air around them. This is a sensation. Not that. You can perceive their form, perhaps even as you move them around. Can you also go within your hands, through the layers of skin, blood, vessels, tendons, and into an appreciation of the cells around and through and within the bones, blood and tissue of this living hand?

Appreciate the empty spaces around the hand. Allow the emptiness within the hand, between structure, between and within each element. Experience the emptiness within and between the cells, within the water. Know that these molecules will soon return to the elemental basis of the universe, unowned by you. Also the body – this quintessence of dust – is a composed form which will decompose. Just as moment by moment we are composing and decomposing as living cells. Just as each time we go to sleep, we die to ourselves and are born again.

The emptiness is always there, containing it all, including the greatest refinement of particles. This emptiness is inherent to our existence.

Emptiness is ubiquitous, all pervasive, almighty, eternal and infinite. Everything that was, is and will ever be is supported and forgiven within this sublime, absolute dimension.

7

Emptiness is Not Nothing

"Just because it is unperceivable, inconceivable and unknowable doesn't mean it can be rejected."

It is emptiness that allows conception, physical life and death. It is emptiness that allows expansion and receptivity. It is emptiness that exists in the space between transient forms – or two sides of polarity – allowing them to blend into one and for something new to be born.

Emptiness permits consciousness to fuse with awareness and for both to expand beyond the furthest reaches, or to focus on one simple atom. Emptiness is the source of creation. It is the inspiration of scientists. It allows all things to exist in order to be witnessed and observed.

Our fears around the perceptive power of emptiness are what cause us to reject life, and also to try to reject what we misunderstand as the rejecter of life.

And in our fall out of emptiness into form which seduces us into believing it is the ultimate truth, we swaddle ourselves with identities, composed of experience to which we become increasingly addicted, and coloured and tailored by our conditioned minds. This is me. This is me. This is who I am. This is my essential being. I can own it forever. This being, not the other. When we reject inherent emptiness, we begin to create our reality, not on the basis of beauty or service, but according to the agenda of our wounds. There emerges a growing sense of inner despair – which bizarrely we name as 'emptiness'.

This is why so often individuals need to come to a position of 'nothing left to lose' before they can begin to live for real.

8

Who Do We Think We Are?

"The greatest gift we can offer ourselves is the gift of allowing the perceptive power of emptiness."

We swaddle the vulnerability of our nakedness with layers of 'somebody', changing robes and fantasies within our striving to get more, to fill the gap, the sense of lack, and this nagging sense that part (or most) of us is inherently empty.

Everyone on earth can believe in the inherent reality of this separate person we have composed. And yet, in our greatest success and glory we begin to starkly understand that we are not that. We can feel incredibly unseen – because at source we are not perceivable. We are standing behind an incredible screen projecting our face on ten-foot billboards and we are unnoticed, unseen and incredibly alone.

Does anyone remember I am here?

When the Dalai Lama spoke in Tel Aviv in 2006, he was able to accomplish the most familiar and easy sense of intimacy with over 2000 people at once. There was none of the tension of fame and glory, just a sense of recognition and easy familiarity.

Much of what he said seemed to be common sense. Yet there was a wisdom which continues to sink through the layers of being, even years after the event. This wisdom emerges not only from what he said, but the naturalness of who he was. There was simply no 'stuff', no mask, no fear and no division between him and the audience.

At a certain stage, the Dalai Lama stopped speaking to the crowded hall, looked at their faces, and then theatrically followed their gaze to the giant video screens of his own image on the right and on the left. He started to laugh, and looked down at his own body. "Which one of them is the real me?" he asked the audience. In that moment, we were all the real him.

The more we believe in the inherent reality of the stuff and status we acquire, the more we swaddle our pure life, our inherent, unaffected freedom and purity, and the more we suffer. Out of this suffering, perception through emptiness begins to tell a tale which can be sound like a mockery at our illusions, yet which contains the supportive strength of inner truth. Who do we think we are?

Thanks to the all-pervasive emptiness, and the cynical knowledge that it was all anyway just a show, we can allow our personalities to evolve in support of deeper need, while uncovering a location in our deeper purpose.

Yet these swaddles, these high fashion personality garments, these pauper's rags or suits of armour at some stage anyway start to rearrange themselves into the shrouds of old age, possibly composed of how we think we might be remembered after we have gone. We begin to fight for that, lest others out of our control recompose who we are when we are helplessly decomposing. The illusions are surrendering to the welcome of emptiness, and we try to give those illusions a fixed place in history.

The greatest gift we can offer ourselves is the gift of allowing the perceptive power of emptiness. When we begin to perceive through form as transience, existence itself begins to shine and the depths of purpose. This is a source of strength, comfort and sacred safety in which our choices are truly liberated to be taken from a position beyond fear. Out of emptiness, the needed form remerges which is of service to the unified whole, which is who we are.

We are the existence which is manifesting through it all, perhaps itself evolving; an inseparable particle of the living universe which is learning all that can be learned through creation in unconditional service to the whole.

This is the gift of life.

9

Emptiness Brings Life

"This is the dimension out of which miracles can occur."

An immediate impact of the initiation of the perceptive power of emptiness is a quickening of vitality. Experience becomes wider, broader and more alive. Each form, thought, feeling and vision seems to become empowered with a new vitality. Some begin to 'see' energy. Others are shocked by an exquisite sense of calm and universal intimacy. Layers of fear that have long not been applicable to any immediate threat are released.

Also, the experience of being physically and energetically alive can become extremely potent. This can take time for the nervous system to integrate. Move gently.

Part of the reason for the great enlivening caused by perception through emptiness is that many of the hooks and conditions that have limited us until now become released. This includes the limitations we could have placed on the scope of our consciousness and awareness.

All the layers of our experience becomes less dense, and more easy to release, which means that we can begin to move in a fast process of unpeeling illusions that can no longer define who we are.

It is as if our own bodies and the density of physical matter become softer and looser. We can see through walls (at least our interior walls). We can even walk through them.

At the same time, there is a release of stress about our place in the various worlds (physical, emotional, social, familial, mental, and spiritual). We are here – in the here and now, attending life. There is no longer a conflict. We are a manifesting miracle.

10

Emptiness and Liberation

"The suffering has no separate self that it could possess us."

Everything that you know, think, feel or experience – everything that comes into your feeling from heaven, earth or the depth of the physical body – this is not ultimately who you are. It is the means through which you are manifesting, but it does not define you.

You are something far more precious, exquisitely beautiful and miraculous.

Yet, as long as we have not realized significant areas of our human state, to the depth, those blind energies have a grip – disguised as aspects of our identity.

Core fears or suffering of rejection or loss can cause us to resist letting go of our hidden habitual states, leading to a clinging to their truth as the final definition of 'reality'.

Yet, all we need to do is to realize these states through softness, loving kindness and acceptance. Within the realization we can accept that they are not who we are; they are illusions which have limited incarnation. We are not the suffering. The suffering has no separate self that it could possess us. We are so much more expansive than pain or fear that we can contain the suffering of the universe and move on unscathed.

In emptiness, nothing is taken away. This means that in rejecting suffering or forbidden aspects of our universe, we are simply hiding them in the emptiness. We will not be free until these divided parts of ourselves – invested with energy – are realized as part of the whole. And when the suffering is transformed, its lessons are not forgotten. Everything that has been consciously experienced is recorded by the Witness.

These latent states or energies can hang like thick shrouds over our essence with such a sense of permanence that we could assume that they are part of the given, permanent, stable atmosphere of life; that this pain is part of the inherent 'truth' of the universe.

From this perspective, we could believe that humanity is eternally cursed with original sin – bringing with it shame, condemnation and banishment. Yet in this, we take a concept to ourselves banish the Garden of Eden from the human state. We not only give these energies a sense of ultimate truth, we give them universality – moving with them as if they were intransient, infinite and eternal.

We can be highly responsive to sudden afflictions of suffering, but to these core states (such as assumed unworthiness or original sin) we can be blind and deaf. We live as if they are an essential part of who we are, and who everyone is. We give them more reality than our own existence.

In our daily lives, this can lead to a forgetting of the universal energies of love and peace. Both can begin to seem a fantasy that needs to be constructed, or imposed. This has quite a drastic effect on human relations, within couples and even on the macro level between nations.

While discomfort at the cusp of expression – such as anger – demands immediate attention, these core states can only be seen, experienced and unpeeled through the development of our faculties of perception, especially through the active integration of perception through emptiness.

For a while, we might not know or be able to sense who we are anymore. But the answer will come when our last fence is fallen, as an existential blessing from an infinite source.

I I

Active: Realization

"This is the perpetual reality check on human living."

The active, assertive perception through emptiness brings with it
a process of self-realization. We move with purity of the witness
and the heart of observation into the midst of states we have long
believed as permanent – states which are inextricably bound to
our belief systems.

In a sense, all the reasons NOT to be free to manifest in
physical form come forward like a line of three-dimensional
horror shows. You think everything is unreal? Is THIS horror
unreal? There can follow a gut-wrenching experience, or even a
period in a tangible projected state in which we experience our
deepest horrors such as abandonment and betrayal. It can be like
a dark night of the soul which continues for days, until we
apprehend that even this threat does not touch who we really are.
When the clouds part again, we can return to the awesome space
of emptiness – and then the next shadow sets in, and the next,
until it is done. Key tools to remember at times like this emerge
from the ancient wisdoms. If you suffer, suffer as a service to the
whole, on behalf of other. Try to release self-interest and move
with unconditional love towards others in your field of
projection.

If you experience the energy of intense cruelty of inhumanity,
experience it as a service. In this field of cruelty, you are there as
an observer. This means that others caught in this space are less
divided. Be patient and move towards yourself with the energy
of softness. Treat yourself with the tenderness with which you
would treat an only child.

In dealing with this unpeeling of deeper layers of denied

feeling and emotion, it is wise to keep an active connection wherever possible with the softness of love in the heart. Mindful breathing is a wonderful tool in keeping ourselves in calm attendance through the passing clouds of suffering and projection.

We must treat these aspects of our emerging experience with great love and softness. If our heart has closed down, then alignment with an attitude of service towards others can also be helpful. Do not suffer for you alone, suffer for all those in pain, on their behalf.

Try to keep structure. But if you find yourself in the midst of a core karmic process, let it take your time. Realizing these latent layers of your false self is probably one of the most important things you will do in your life. The beneficial impact on your whole ability to manifest through joy will be tremendous.

Perception through emptiness can be used directly within the different dimensions of stillness, allowing a refinement. It is perception through emptiness that allows an increasing unity between several dimensions of stillness – allowing all to exist in experience at the same time.

It can open space for an increasing blend between consciousness and awareness and for that blend to take the precise composition needed in the moment.

Emptiness is also a powerful tool in supporting us through the navigation of the spaces between – the rifts between ourselves and others – where so much negative energy tends to be dumped to recompose in demonic, disowned forms. In the healing therapies, perception through emptiness brings a particular connection when laying the hands on the person. It can be almost as if the hand can pass through the body and interact directly within its energetic and physical form – without either having an inherent reality. When used in this manner, it is always wise to invite a synergy between emptiness and awareness, and to move with softness and an awareness of the sacred.

12

Receptive: Permission

"Let the demons show themselves and speak it out."

By definition ultimately permissive, in that it allows every phenomenon appearing on heaven, earth and elsewhere to exist, the receptive power of emptiness tends to evoke the strongest illusions into manifestation.

When you reside within the receptivity of emptiness with another, it can be as if there is an energetic X-ray. Precisely those areas where they are most stuck in their process or where the energy is most dense come forward and begin to talk. As such, they allow themselves involuntarily to be witnessed and observed by you. The receptive power of emptiness allows the deepest 'seeing' of the other.

From the receptivity of emptiness, every expression has its beauty and can take a form, transforming and evolving according to deeper need.

Again, when dealing with others, the energy of emptiness also in receptive form can be quite harsh and polarizing. Our friend can clamp shut, feel invaded, or make you the target of her projections.

As such it is important to keep an active link-up with consciousness (affirm physical form through consciousness, in order to transmit a stability and trust), and with awareness – awareness as a carrier of softness and love, even of appreciation. There is no contradiction in this.

Still: Eternity

"In a society where the chief motivation for action seems to be fear and threat, the experience of the stillness of eternity gives tremendous strength."

Sinking into the depth of emptiness, without receiving or asserting anything, existence is able to expand through a dimension we would like to call the Stillness of Eternity.

A potent source of unending strength residing in this dimension can give the inherent support we need to stand behind cause and effect, and behind the survival issues of physical time, or physical illness.

In this, a new freedom emerges to make real choices for changes in the structure of our life or in the patterns that have held us enslaved. Sometimes it can be as simple as the realization that we are allowed to say "No."

In a society where the chief motivation for action seems to be fear and threat, the experience of the stillness of eternity gives tremendous strength, supporting the integrity of the individual passion to be of service to the whole.

14

The Will

"Thy will is my will."

The cynics were right by the way: emptiness is not entirely empty.

At least, in the dimension of emptiness, it is possible to locate an essential seed which on investigation contains a tremendous passion to evolve through service. The expression of this through the layers of being, understanding and manifestation will be highly precise to the moment and to the individual. However, it is possible to talk a little about this active seed.

Called the Will, this seed is an ingredient positioned within the dimension of emptiness within the coccyx. It contains an unlimited, unconditional wish to evolve. It is expressed in virtually every individual on the planet, young or old. It manifests as a will to make good, to improve, to live and to develop. It is a will that goes beyond personal survival. It gives individuals the ability to sacrifice themselves for the sake of an idea, a principle, or for the sake of the survival of the whole.

This Will generates an energy which moves upwards along the spine, bringing its intention forward for formulation through sensuality, sexuality, the central dimension of the heart, through the mind and consciousness, and connecting upward to the light of spirit, or creative power beyond ourselves and beyond the individual.

It is the will behind the Christian precept of surrender: "Thy Will be done." Yet in practice, although this can lead to a great purification of the Will, it is also our individual will which is done as we move through life. This is one of the miracles of creation. As pure existence, thy will is my will.

15

The Passion

"When suffering is allowed and lived as a service to the whole, there is the birth of passion and a resurrection into the world of form."

Just because we do not have a separate self, and all we experience, feel or do is transient, it doesn't mean life is senseless. It is precisely out of the emptiness that the deepest sense of purpose for an individual human being is born.

Just as the release of consciousness brings forward an intense experience of bliss, and the release of being evokes ecstasy, the energetic experience from the heart of the will is passion.

Passion, as a root word, also means suffering. And within the refined field of emptiness, the two are the same. Christians could take the Passion of Christ as an example of this. When suffering is allowed and lived as a service to the whole, there is the birth of passion and a resurrection into the world of form.

This can be connected with destiny, karma and individual qualities. But as an example, if we have suffered abandonment and abuse, then a passion is also born within the realization of the suffering. This passion is in the first place to be there also for others. This is the opening of empathy.

As we rise into form to the heart dimension, the passion manifests as compassion. Compassion involves the recognition of inter-being – we are together in this suffering or passion with others. Our well-being is interdependent. We dedicate our hearts and energies to service in this field. As it rises to the level of consciousness, wisdom emerges, at a depth which supports understanding of the whole field and the means to give form and structure the service.

16

Unity

"It is in the dense dimension of physical matter that emptiness becomes most apparent."

The soul aspect which pervades as a background to the dimension of emptiness is unity. When I first mention this to students, they are often shocked. Unity? In the root? The idea that it is precisely the 'lower' dimension – all that ugly physical stuff – which is the opening to sacred unity can appear as a paradox. Yet what we know as the 'lowest' dimension – physical matter – is also in some ways the most inviolate, strong and the most suffused with the perpetual sanctity of creation and the emergence of form. It is in the dense dimension of physical matter that emptiness becomes most apparent.

When we contemplate the densest expression of energy available to our perception – the physical world – the world of bones, flesh, cement, mortar and neatly painted asphalt, it becomes clear that there can be no unity which does not contain that. If we excluded the matter of which we are composed as individual humans, it wouldn't be unity but escapism. In truth matter does not divide us: it is the most tangible, physical proof of our unity.

Our physical bodies, alive as they are, are also the clearest declaration of physical unity. They declare it constantly, these bodies, as they drag behind us as we venture forth in our 'higher' process of spiritual development. Loyally, they ground it all. Whether conscious or not, and beyond the furthest reaches of our awareness, these bodies persist as a magnificent composition of universal matter.

Although we can find a thousand reasons why not to think

about it right now, these bodies of ours are also in transformation. We will undergo a death process, and the physical body will be cremated or buried in order to slowly decompose into the elements. Even the fresh air we are breathing is suffused with the particles of bodies of those that have lived and died.

And this is not only a future event. Within the timeless, vertical dimension of the present moment, our physical conception and our decomposition are coexisting. There is no greater proof and fact of the transience of form than our physical flesh and blood, and the hard ground on which it stands.

So potent is this, that when there is sound it vibrates through every molecule and cell of our physical bodies, whether or not we know or like the other people in the room. We are responding in unity to every passing truck, and each whisper from a baby's lips, whether or not we allow it within our awareness or know it within our consciousness. At the heart of matter, we are one. This basis of unity contains the mid-dimension of sentient awareness and the upper dimension of wisdom and peace. It is the infinite empire that allows the stillness of eternity, the stillness of being and the stillness of silence. It is the powerful support to passion, ecstasy and bliss. It is the unending perimeter of self-realization as it turns back towards a refining of enlightenment and awakening.

Dissolving in this soul aspect of unity, behind time and space, within the great and persuasive playing field of creation in the grey space between polarities, we are one.

If we return to the story of the unborn, we notice that in the coming together of two sides of a polarity, man and woman, something new is born: the embryo of all that we are. If this embryo could report, it would be telling that its formation is a kind of vibration, a movement in which it has been separated from the pure atmosphere of peace, love and unity from which it emerged. It would be almost cynical about the division – because it is still composed within peace, love and unity, and it knows the division is transient.

Just as a handful of sand lifted from the seashore is still sand, and knows it can be scattered in all directions across the planet, yet it can never have its 'sandness' taken away, even if every grain were to be spiralled through infinite space. Just as a reflection of light gives light and is composed of light. Just as the water in our bodies and in each individual cell is part of the universal element of water, and when it returns to the ocean will become the ocean. Just in this way, we are an inseparable part of creation as it manifests, moment by moment.

17

The Rifts in Creation

"When we cut rifts between the desirable and undesirable, we are able to justify the most horrific cruelty and to coldly turn away from unspeakable degrees of suffering."

Yet how is it that peace, love and unity can flip over so suddenly to war, hatred and cruelty?

It is important to note that, the moment we begin to move with the realization of unity, we will encounter all the reasons why we cannot be one.

Try talking about oneness or unity to a friend. Notice how they react. Notice how you are reacting. In some ways, unity is one of the most rebellious weapons among us in that it is a direct insult to the status quo of mutually sustained illusion.

Yes we are one. The whole dimension of experience is one – individual and shared, beyond polarity. Yet they murder babies within this unity. That cannot be allowed to exist here. Not the cruelty. Not the genocide. Not Hitler. Not all that evil in the 'other'.

Come to think of it, that complaining neighbour is also on the edge.

Where do we put all that stuff which we are banishing from this brave, new, man-made kidnapping of the idea of socially acceptable unity?

We know from a place preceding knowing that all appearance of division is transient – it is not an absolute truth. As such, we tend to move perception away from uncontainable cruelty or trauma, into the safety of emptiness – the eternal space we know so well.

Within the splitting apart and divisions inherent in creation, between the man and the woman, or between one cell and another, there is a kind of trauma or original suffering.

Just as when lovers come together in the purity of unity, they must later separate and feel the stark pain of division, so does new life experience a bitterness, agony and longing to return to its seamless state within the whole.

With the birth of new life, there is a division through which space is opened between all phenomena – that very space which makes creation possible.

These cracks in creation run like rifts between us: between one body and the next, between my reality and your reality, between one country and the rest of the world. They can be visualized as networks of light, in which form represents the shadow or the darkness.

They also run through our whole experience of being alive. Between our spiritual and material experience; between our minds and our hearts; between each word we think and the intent out of which the thought was formed.

Beyond the natural rifts there are also rifts which are a result of human freedom or learning. We use our freedom to structure and create forms of marvellous beauty. Yet we also use it to support our survival – a movement which is often generated by the blind logic of fear.

Thus, through the cutting of rifts between desirable and undesirable experience, we are able to justify the most horrific cruelty and to turn away from unspeakable degrees of suffering.

As we increasingly develop the art of perception through emptiness, many of these rifts disappear in an increasing movement towards simplicity. Remaining rifts can become our highways through living experience as we dedicate ourselves to become of service to the whole. When emptiness is recognized as our inherent basis, the rifts become channels of service.

When we begin living through emptiness, repressed emotion and abandoned parts of human experience can at first come to the foreground. For generations, we have been throwing unwanted parts of collective experience into the emptiness – which pervades and underlies every split and division. Perhaps we believed that there these unwanted phenomena would cease to exist.

Yet these bodies of pain continue, forever created and quite forsaken, irrespective of our conscious mind or the soft expansion of our awareness through the field of form. Here we will find the experiences we have thrown into the rifts of emptiness – perhaps as children, when we had no other choice. Here, we will find these injured forms manifesting themselves in palpable reality of experience before us, telling us that because they are still there, we can never be free and humanity will never be whole.

Until now, psychologists have located these phenomena in unconscious mind. If it begins affecting our thoughts and behaviour, it becomes, in their terminology, subconscious, and certainly a mental affliction.

It is a convenient definition – that which is 'not conscious', that which is not within the control of the mind. But it neglects the deeper responsibility to explore what is beyond consciousness – as if it were hardly relevant.

It begs the question: when there is cruelty beyond bounds and agony that no mortal can contain at that moment in physical form, is it ever going to be in the control of the mind or of consciousness? Can these experiences of suffering be realized as delusional, without a deeper realization of the illusion of all experience?

Consciously, in practice, we forgive, but we never forget. Yet not to forget is not enough; we need to remember, in the sense of inviting the trapped parts of experience back into membership of the whole, back within the human unity.

We know that these horrors are there, in the emptiness. We can jump over rift after rift, but at some stage, some moment when we are least aware – in sleep or when we think we are enlightened – one of the wounded forms will raise its head from the empty expanse, wailing through our interior night that it is alive, on the edges of the emptiness. Full of living atmosphere and in total contradiction to the conscious mind we will hear its haunting voice saying: "I AM HERE."

Do we push it away, because we are already healed? It is there, but we are not that. We are in unity. It is an illusion, a part of the pain body. It is not here. It is a lie.

Or do we pull it out of the rift and off that part of ourselves where it has already attached and throw the experience at another human being in the form of projection – back to our client, to the world, the government, our ex?

Are we able to begin to let ourselves be responsive and to become responsible for the shared suffering inherent in creation?

Can we let the demons enter the windows of our perception, perhaps to find that they are composed of particles of universal love, peace and unity? Even, that they are but wounded children rejected into the night? Can we welcome them and open the door?

People who have been through the most painful and horrific experiences of physical, emotional and spiritual cruelty know this: there is a sacred safety in the emptiness.

The emptiness cannot be tortured and abused. The emptiness rejects nothing and no one. The emptiness is stronger than every element of horror. It is the backdrop which supports a process of realization. Although all this horrific manifestation exists within my experience, I am not that. Infused with particles of peace, love and unity, emptiness alone has the power to unhook the worst nightmare from the appearance of definitive truth. In this, compassion moves from the heart dimension and makes a healing invitation towards the abandoned forms in the emptiness to re-enter the human dimension. It is a kind of miracle how quickly these abandoned children that looked like ghouls can become at one again within the family of the heart.

Are we ready with our will, hearts and minds to become part of the collective process of healing the ruptures born within creation through the inclusion of all form within the interwoven human dimensions of love, peace and unity?

Are we ready to be free?

18

Existence and Her Golden Chains

"The opposite sex is a first field where issues of 'otherness' and separation emerge."

When we first begin perceiving through emptiness, there is a clarification of who you are as pure existence. Nakedly, perception takes place and moves through a dimension in which even the densest matter seems to attain fluidity in the way in which it is experienced.

Yet there is also something else going on beyond the subject of experience and this takes place around existence. Glued to the Observer and the Witness are certain core attitudes. They could be there from habit, or they could be inborn. Yet they do seem to differ from one person to another. These chains begin to be reflected back by the emptiness and one by one they fall away as no longer necessary. They are subtle, but they restrict the freedom of movement and manifestation of existence in physical form.

Such attitudes could reflect ambition, impatience, caution, recklessness, righteousness or superiority. There could be an imbalance of action or effort and receptivity, which can generate frustration. Often they are connected to wounds around the gender divide, and the separation of female from male. As humans, gender is a core division and lasts as long as the body. It is one of the basic human polarities. As such, the opposite sex is a first field where issues of 'otherness' and separation emerge.

At first, because of the emptiness, it can appear that these atmospheres derived from our attitudes fill the whole space. This can create quite a suffering and can send tremors through the nervous system.

This atmosphere is so fine, intangible, and intimately hooked into the one that is experiencing it that it takes on the flavour of absolute reality. This clarity of perception of betrayal or unworthiness cannot be illusion, can it?

Could it be possible to continue to trust this emptiness that brings our shadows to life with full vitality and horror? It is in our power to use the authenticity of your awareness, the light of consciousness, and the refined rationality of our minds supported by deeper wisdom to differentiate and explore these perceptive filters between existence and emptiness.

It is an adventure which will often entail the opposite polarity of the attitude. For example, an attitude of superiority could well be present as a contra to a less visible sense of unworthiness. Selfishness could be present as a result of a personality that has been wounded in its natural form.

The result will be an unchaining of existence from the limitations of attitude.

Don't be disheartened: there is sacred safety in the emptiness available in each moment in the beautiful, love-charged, indestructible presence of the existence which is who you are.

19

Disillusion

"When our future collapses and our past seems to be a lie, then where do we stand? Where is the truth that will never fail us?"

In popular language, disillusion, like disappointment, is in the 'dis' category, along with disgrace, disapproval, disgust, disrespect or disappointment. Disillusionment is commonly understood as a state of depression, even verging on despair. It can represent the collapse of hopes, dreams and expectations and even the undressing of love – the belief in absolute coupledom or soulmates as a fantasy.

In general, we like to control and choose where we will be disillusioned and which illusions must stand as truth. We like that, but we don't yet know how to master it.

Perception through emptiness is quite ruthless. Whether we come there through choice or through the disillusionment or breakdown in belief systems, it will often impact far more of our illusory world than the loss immediately before us.

When our future collapses and our past seems to be a lie, then where do we stand? Where is the truth that will never fail us? Those who have been enlightened in the dimension of the heart can suffer a horrible disillusionment and a momentary collapse in confidence in their ability to be of service to others. This can show in burnout, an undirected jealousy or a deep pain of rejection. The drive towards unity can begin to feel more like an overpowering death wish underwritten by a deep rage towards the universe for the brutal act of creation and the senselessness of the suffering it is causing.

Does it really matter? Does matter?

Be aware that this rage at illusion of our most sacred purpose is polarizing. If our most cherished moments of experiencing humanity are illusory, if everything we think, feel and know is inherently transient, then the suggestion is that it has no value – you have lost your purpose or reason for living.

Yet, notice that what is coming forward is the voice of wounded consciousness or the subtle layers of ego. Either it is all real and I am absolutely special or nothing matters at all. It's her or me. This shows a core personality structure of either-or – the deep dualism of being alive.

Between consciousness and emptiness, the resolution and answer is at the depths of the heart and in the still awareness that can contain the coexistence of a multitude of perspectives. Our world is made up of transient phenomena or illusions which have no inherent reality. Yet this lesser reality is of tremendous importance as part of the absolute purpose of existence.

All we do, think, feel or achieve is inherently transient. At the same time, each and every particle of our experience and manifestation is precious to the whole – as precious and sacred as creation itself. We can realize our unity, without losing our individuality. Our process is precious to creation. Our composition moment by moment is individually and magnificently unique. To be truly special does not negate the specialness of the other, and it does not mean we are divided. Our individuality simple enriches the unity.

The only belief we need to release in order to allow this miracle is the illusion of our absolute separation, the belief in a separate 'ME' which must be defended.

The process of realization on any given golden thread of your process will culminate with a fresh degree of freedom in which you become able to choose the illusions most worthwhile for your lifetime in service to the manifestation of your existence. Those illusions, invested with authenticity, will always be of service to the whole.

Why should we care about what we cannot ultimately understand?
Because we are here.
Why does it matter?
Because we are one.

20

Masters of Form

"We can become more intensely individual and more securely part of the whole than ever before."

The magic of mastering form results from the realization of the transient nature of all form and its emptiness of a separate self. This realization brings us into expanding acceptance of inherent unity – in which the divisions within us are no longer absolute, but manifold expressions of one source.

Undoing lifetimes of conditioning of separation as absolute takes time, and the ego and other structures of self will fight back. Yet to sit among others and to truly move into the clear experience of unity is deeply liberating and, by degrees, shockingly obvious. Our existence which we have swaddled for so long is in its purity the same as theirs. Our consciousness, when unhooked from identity and expanding, is a shared field, and nothing needs to be defended. Our awareness as a shared plane of being, undefined by what is happening, what is resolving, or the weather of feeling, it is one source, uniquely and individually expressed.

In this pure individuality lies the mastery of form. There has never been and will never be another expression or manifestation of form as you in this moment. This is true on the level of physical time: the precise combination of your unique genealogy with environment at this age of the body and its organs, past and future.

This is true on the level of sentient time: the formulation of love in this moment as it uncovers the unique combination of energy resolving itself through pain and joy, all observed by its source.

It is also the case at the throne of the individual – the level of consciousness. This identity, this knowledge, this special process of understanding and this unique, individual wisdom is entirely new and enriching the universal plane of knowledge.

As such, form, although it is transient and has no separate existence, is precious beyond belief. Our ability to release, evolve and respond according to its highest purpose is the greatest service we can offer ourselves, humanity and the universe.

Part of our attachment to form arises from a latent belief that if we do not have an agenda for it – if we are not in control – then it will collapse to dust, or will possibly become destructive. This is not true. In the release of form into emptiness, there is the resurrection of a finer form, one attuned to the highest needs and beyond our limited agenda. This affinity between universal will and individual expression means that the degree of suffering and waste is minimalized. The form we take manifests precisely according to the highest needs of the moment.

It is important to affirm that through the release of form in this manner, we do not become non-individual and formless. On the contrary, we can become more intensely individual and more securely part of the whole than ever before. This is because the fight between our ideas of individuality and the universal whole is ended: we are embraced and supported in all our moments.

The latent, unchallenged belief that individuality is somehow a negation of unity is an absurdity. Through the liberation of the individual, the whole becomes more enriched. Through the acceptance of unity and the whole, the individual shines more brightly. Precision in details of diversity allows the refinement, development and the most exquisite evolution of the whole tapestry of life.

V
Here Am I

Our Friend called Fear

"The watchmen at the door are not our captors."

While the centre of the head is a primary seat of consciousness, our consciousness moves strongly through the solar plexus region – registering as attraction, repulsion, excitement and fear. This dimension is where we put out our energetic feelers into the world with one base agenda – to physically survive.

Yet physical survival often depends on being socially accepted, on being fed and nurtured, and in not becoming insane in the eyes of the world, so this simple dictate 'survive' can have a tremendous impact on the way we think, on how we express ourselves, and on the choices we make.

Fear is a natural part of physical life. It is connected to the instinct to survive, which in turn is connected to our ability to adapt socially. We have ample ability to construct stories in the mind. If we miss this, our parents, schools and societies will supply us with category after category of threats and conse- quences if we do not bow to the imagined authority of this demigod called fear.

The command: "BE AFRAID" can be so extreme that in some cases, if we are not fearful, then we are seen as traitors of the whole tribe. Take our collective attitude to the war against terror, for example, shortly after a major terrorist event.

Beyond the basic, collective fears shared by all mortal beings, we find ourselves webbed in with elaborate constructions of fear, based on the fear of fear – often of a pain or trauma that happened long ago and is no longer an immediate threat.

These fears can additionally block other natural instincts, emotions or feelings, such as anger, or grief. In many ways, fear has become the silent gatekeeper to physical embodiment.

Bypassing feeling, fear triggers our minds to build stories that form elaborate shields of justification against authentic feeling or experience. Even spirituality can fall into this trap by encouraging a rejection of physical form or emotional authenticity (let's 'transcend' the whole nightmare of human life).

This can complicate the manifestation of authentic existence to such an extent that in the end, still unsatisfied with the small, solid, safe space left to us, fear begins to attack itself as the enemy and becomes panic or anxiety. Even behind these battalions and grouped within our private tribe, there is still no safety, because anyway these physical bodies are frail and will wilt around us.

In addition to panic attacks or anxiety, repressed fear can create dramatic projections on the world and on others. We can become fixated on a person, a cause, or the suffering in a neighbouring country. We can begin to seek safety in irrational places, people or beliefs. We can find ourselves in the grip of a compulsive need to 'know' stuff. Worse, it can lead to an aggressive insistence on being an absolute authority on 'the reality'.

Some noble people, in their wounded passion, delve into 'fixing' the outer world with a passion that decries its inner wound. This can lead to psychosis and varying degrees of mental illness.

For many, severe anxiety can be a turning point in self-development. The same fear arising to ensure safety begins to create a hell so vivid that there is nothing to lose but fear itself.

We can fear death so much that we create and recreate a thousand situations in which we die. We have a compulsion to do this, from a place of survival, as if in this way we could ensure that none of them will ever happen. At a certain stage, having died a thousand horrific deaths, we might wake up to the understanding that, when we die, we will only die once. The same method can become our torture chamber for fears of abandonment or betrayal.

Fear is there to safeguard physical life, yet in order to truly live in safety, we need to unhook our fears as the authority on our thoughts, feelings and choices. We need to realize physical life as non-absolute. In this way, we unhook physical life as the first authority, thus allowing our existence to truly come to life in the physical.

The way to do this is not to repress fear but to give it space. This allows movement. Liberated fear is alive and appropriate to the moment, giving the precise signals when we need to act, stirring up the needed adrenalin and opening the instinctive resources.

As we find we are able to release unnecessary layers of fear, the mind becomes clearer, stillness begins to emerge, and the space is created for the real work of coming to life.

The more we become aware of our fear so that it responds in real time, the less we need to project stories onto the world, and the less controlling we become towards ourselves and others. Deeper control is gained through an ability to contain experience and work with fear.

Fear is just experience. And it is the gargoyles of fear that guard the gates of liberation, on all levels and at all stages of inner development. Yet no matter how frightening the appearance, our existence may pass unscathed. Deep down, in our sacred home of emptiness, we know this, yet we get entangled in our wish to preserve or control form.

At first, allowing the energy of fear might not give answers in itself. There could be layers of fear locked around trauma. There could be a long-term pattern of fear or resulting addiction that has created quite a wasteland of depression around the area of the heart, leading to freezing of feeling. These areas of frozen feeling can take some sentient time to arouse back into life. Yet when we turn and face our fears, they are the ones that run.

The lion's share of any process of awakening will work through the structures of fear we have built on and around this basic, instinctual fear – the fear to be physically alive. The key is to have the courage to turn towards and not away – surrendering to the fear itself. It is a leap of faith and it is a choice for deeper mastery. The watchmen at the door are not our captors.

Fear is a gatekeeper of experience and, in some ways, it is the prison master. It is imperative to realize that this inner jailor is in fact part of ourselves. We always had the keys. It is not a jailor but a preserver of form. All we need to do is to stand in that which gives rise to form, and our prison becomes a palatial home.

The first flash of the experience of fear is apprehension. Through the cracks of our sleep and our habitual, close-knit mental patterns we glimpse an outer space, an 'other'. The 'other' threatens change. We believe we are not safe.

In its purest form, nothing exists without universal purpose. The collective fear of change is so all encompassing that it could be said to be a meta fear embracing the four collective fears of classical psychology: the fear of death, the fear of illness, the fear of insanity and the fear of sexuality. The fear of change could also be expressed as the fear of life, death or transformation.

Evolution, growth and creation takes place in a dance between change, preservation and consolidation. A sculptor carefully begins to chisel the curves of the nostril of his master portrait. He is effecting change. Yet he must always hold the stability of the mass of stone. If he moves too fast there could be a total disintegration. Social and political systems evolve according to a series of reforms, responding to need, each reform built on the consolidation of the status quo in the system that went before. Change is dependent on stability.

A plant grows by degrees, out of its own form, not in opposition to its template. It can grow fast, but the speed is partly dependant on the maintenance of the balance of inner form and strength.

Change confronts us with new experience – experience that needs to be integrated with our minds, beliefs, personalities and feelings. It could also need integration with the way we stand in the world and our direction. Fear says, "Slow down."

Fear also awakens the whole system to a state of sensitivity. There is change. There is a need to respond. Survival depends on it. Inner growth depends on it.

In order to respond to change, it is necessary to be alert, so natural fear stirs up an increased awakening of awareness and consciousness – perceptive tools directly invested in responding to life. Awareness scouts the field for change. The awakened Witness positions the 'I' on the field of awareness. It is directed to move through awareness according to the deeper needs of our condition. All of this is observed from a timeless space of pure awareness.

There can be a need to remove impediments to the transcendental aspects of peace, love and unity. These impediments are found in the areas where we are suffering, or where we cling to false ideas or beliefs of self or who we are – ideas which no longer serve our highest interests. Whether it is a matter of survival or new opportunity, fear is an activator.

Moving through an apprehension of need, fear brings with it the energy needed to give wings to self-development, or to slow it down, and consolidate what has been learned.

As such, fear is no enemy, in its natural form. It is a stimulus to awakening, enlightenment and self-realization. It escorts us to the opening of the source of existence and vanishes without a trace. In manifesting yourself as a human being, fear can be your advisor and watchman, yet it should not be master of your choices.

In real time, it is the instinctive energy that activates the clarity of mind, power and responsiveness that saves lives. It is also connected with psychic abilities and the wonderful energetic web that connects the whole manifold field of individual humans. Pure fear brings pure energy, and this is an energy which can be purified and used in service of the whole.

We should surely be at peace with this fellow traveller called fear. And though she might sing, we should maintain a careful observation of her in choosing our direction.

2

Love and Rejection

"Rejection is the mother of all illusions."

One of the greatest fears – moving beyond the fear of change – is the fear of rejection.

Change could be welcomed if we did not fear our division from the whole. This fear is a child of creation – as every act of creation involves division or a break from unity, and the reformation of a new unity. This is true on the cellular level and throughout all dimensions of perception.

The healing factor in the movement behind consciousness to the position of witness is that choice no longer become exclusive in an absolute sense: to choose a direction is not to eternally negate the other option.

On the level of awareness, the healing factor is found in the position of the observer: even though we might be in the midst of intense suffering, pain and cruelty, this too is seen, from behind and from within. I am in suffering, but the suffering does not define me.

On the level of existence, the healing factor emerges in the realization of unity and the indestructability of existence. Rejection is seen as an absurdity.

Yet, in on our way towards these three perceptive origins and in our movement into the unified space within that, the pain of rejection can emerge as if it were an inherent part of the human state. We are thrown out of Eden. We strive to return to a state which was prior to what we share now. Humanity seems to be, as it were, cursed by God.

This latent, collective belief is an originating cause of the veiling of our windows of perception; it is behind much of our suffering, and of the blind cruelty we inflict on others.

On the positive side, the experience of being rejected or metaphorically crucified can be of great service to a process in which all that we believed we needed to defend is released. Through surrendering to the cruelty of others, without resistance, the deeper magic emerges which is the miracle of who we truly are.

By degrees, our reactivity to human conflict transforms to compassion and responsibility as we perceive this cruelty as a reflection of the state of suffering and pain which holds others in its grasp.

Rejection, like shame, is a hot potato. Individuals pass it on as rapidly as they can to the other, or to another tribe or group. There are very few people who have learned to contain its pain and to let the cycle of rejection resolve within their own field of experience. To do this is of tremendous service.

To be of service to process arising out of the I AM HERE teachings, it is necessary to add some reflections on rejection.

There is as much love in the universe as any individual can physically or emotionally contain. When the doors of love open towards us, it is we who cry "stop" as the experience can be of complete dissolution. We ourselves put borders to this powerful love, dosing ourselves according to the measure of our fears, and trying to structure it with our minds by hooking it onto individuals or places. This is a process of evolution and manifestation in which humanity is developing as a physical channel of love. In its natural form, it is not rejection of the universe.

The universe has not rejected us from the elated spiritual, and it never rejects us. We need have no fight with the source of all life, or, in essence, with whom we really are. This is the last frontier of peace.

The world of form, colour and manifestation is happening at core as a result of vibration. I am a vibration. Each manifesting entity and each atom is a pattern of vibration.

In this lifetime, you are a song – a song sung by your existence, which is existence itself. A singer is not rejecting the song. It is a highly unique articulation. As each rhythm passes and each melody moves to the next, it is gone. The true mystery and beauty of the song can only be truly received through surrender in the here and now. When we surrender to music through the levels of perception, it is as if we are the instruments which are being played by the vibration. There is no rejection in this. No individual can ever reject another, they can only try and destroy the form, operating from a position of agonized illusion. Rejection is the mother of all illusions.

3

Trilogy in Motion

"The sentient window of awareness and the absolute window of emptiness are the perceptive floors on which consciousness itself is resting."

The purpose of separating the three perceptive windows is not to leave them separate or to create rifts between our head, heart and physical basis. The purpose is to come to a deeper, refined and more empowered integration in order to remove the rubble and chains around the physical, intellectual and spiritual beauty manifesting existence.

The intention is to deliberately bring light to an imbalance and restriction in how we are habitually employing our means of perception. It is as if consciousness has won the show, and the wondrous windows through awareness and emptiness are used as by-products taken for granted but never fully realized as inherent aspects of human form. As we begin exploring the three windows, the rapid development and quickening of under-standings and processes make it clear that the sentient window of awareness and the absolute window of emptiness are the perceptive floors on which consciousness itself is resting. No window of perception will ever negate the others. The opening of awareness will lead to the greater expansion of the mind and clarity of consciousness. The opening of emptiness can encourage a significant increase in precision of mind and silence beyond verbal thought, and new revelations of emotional states or areas of inner pain in the dimension of awareness. Consciousness itself is the initiator of explorations through awareness and emptiness: it is the great awakener and to some degree the protective escort through processes of inner development.

In denying the independent perceptive power of awareness and emptiness, we find we cast huge parts of human experience into the wilderness. We create rifts between us, cover the horrors we fear with perceptive blind spots. We close down our ability to become responsible, as there are certain processes or feelings that we reject from existence. We divide ourselves from our natural being as living forms within creation, and the manifestation of that, and we divide our children from their own chance to manifest existence. Our misunderstandings, misapprehensions and the fears of that which we have rejected lead us to construct whole belief systems and educational cultures to ensure an illusory sense of unity and safety.

Investment in the development and refinement of awareness and sentience, especially in how we relate to our inner world, has a direct healing impact on our inner lives, on our relationships and on our environment.

The conscious mind can follow this experience, and cooperate by coming to deepening degrees of understanding and wisdom. Our beliefs can cooperate through choices we make to let them soften, evolve and surrender. Yet awareness leads the way, with the conscious mind following.

This choice, to allow ourselves to experience awareness as the leader – often even without the conscious mind needing to name or explain experience – in itself creates a deepening of experience and the opening of a process in which energetic blocks begin to move and to release more vitality.

When we find ourselves entangled with experience, or identifying with it, then the perceptive power of emptiness comes into play. What would happen if we just drop it? We stay there, in the same area of anger or fear, but perceive it as energetic phenomena through the eyes of emptiness. We find ourselves even more curious, as the experience changes form, expands or focusses, and begins to tell us its inner story. Drop it again but keep looking. It is opening into a process of liberation in which nothing is lost.

Consciousness and awareness follow the experience and process it. But they are not the experience. The experience is a song which will reach its conclusion.

These are just some examples of how the trilogy of perception moves once we open the three windows of perception and our existence begins to expand and explore the miracle of pure humanity.

Such is the structure of the perceptive pyramid: to truly move to the perspective of the observer at the source of pure awareness, the witness of consciousness needs to surrender itself; and to truly move into the infinite power of existence within the manifold unity of emptiness, the observer needs to dissolve or melt into the absolute, unconditional reality of existence, releasing the perspective of the heart.

4

The Trilogy and Sexuality

"Sexuality moves us through the trilogy of perception. As such, it opens the frontiers of creation and destruction."

Sexuality is a highly important part of our manifestation as human beings. Such is its power to unite, expose and open a process, that it has been abused by dynamics of fear, control and pretence.

A subject for a future book, it is nevertheless worthwhile to share how the three dimensions of human perception are reflected through our sexuality. As stated earlier, the physical limitation of gender does not determine an energetic or experiential limitation. Although as a man, the male aspect might be in the foreground, the female aspect is still accessible, and its integration critical to inner growth. Likewise for women: in the acquaintance and healing of the inner male aspects, a woman is able to come into her full strength without any compromise to her present position as a human female. Sexuality moves us through the trilogy of perception.

So it is with orgasm. The male and female orgasms reflect the upward and downward circulation through the central column which is inherent to deeper processes of inner growth.

The male orgasm begins with an attraction through the seeing of consciousness, through this penetrating portal of perception that inquires into the 'other' which in heterosexual couples would be the female. When a conscious connection is attained, the energy falls down to the heart level. The man 'falls' in love – at least for that moment. The dimension of awareness and sentience opens. Then energy begins to fall and incarnate to the root basis. Here, there is a build-up of pressure, demanding release. In the moment before orgasm, the man touches pure emptiness – as if nothing is happening. Then the tidal wave occurs.

The female orgasm picks up the circulation. At first only accessible in the broad field of sensuality, longing and need to be 'seen', the female orgasm involves a general powerful build-up in the area of the G-spot. This expands beyond time and space and through and beyond the male and female polarity.

At the moment of pure emptiness – when everything becomes purely commonplace as if nothing is happening – her orgasm is initiated, from the physical detail of body in an upward movement through the central column.

It rises through the field of sensuality, in which all form emerges, and passes to the dimension of the heart. Here, the physical orgasm becomes an experience of ecstasy. If she continues allowing expansion through emptiness, the orgasm will then rise to the conscious dimension in the head, and she will experience a refined bliss.

The energy travels upward and circulates through the two in an increasing blend towards unity. At a certain stage, it becomes clear that circulation is happening in both directions, through the male and female aspects of each partner.

5

A Revolving Torus

"Within this hollow channel is the inherent unity of creation and inherent eternity – a space behind, within and outside of time."

Without violating the highly precise world of mathematics and geometry, the visual image of the four-dimensional torus (or hypertorus) gives a close indication of how perception moves through our energy field in trilogy.

The torus is like a bagel, in constant revolution inside-out, through the empty canal in the centre. Through the central channel of the energy system, or physically, along the spine to the centre of the skull, all three aspects of perception are found in purity.

The hollow central channel is emptiness itself, allowing rapid movement of consciousness and awareness through the vertical column and out both ends. Within this hollow channel is inherent unity of creation and inherent eternity – a space behind, within and outside of time.

Yet this emptiness expands and retracts creating a movement we recognize as passion – a passion to allow life, rejecting nothing. The expansion or retraction of emptiness could be understood as changes within the frequencies of consciousness and awareness, but perhaps not. Without vulgarizing science, it is worthwhile to note that physicists are talking about the expansion of the universe at an exponential rate – an expansion they have associated with a mysterious force for now labelled 'dark energy'.

The next experiential layer of the central channel is the layer of awareness. Abundantly happy to the point of ecstasy, this is like the diffusing line of clear grey where light particles penetrate darkness. Beyond dualism, it is nevertheless the synergetic space where polarity comes together.

The closest layer to the physical is that of consciousness – the experience of bliss occurring within the meeting point with physical matter and the independent awakening of existence in physical form.

In four dimensions, this ring torus revolves inside and outside of itself around a central axis. Moving outside time and space as we habitually know it, in terms of perception, this means that even the sensation of a butterfly at one moment resting on the outer perimeter of our consciousness or awareness will register also through the central column, inside-out. It also suggests that the opening of the portals of perception at the depth and the accessing of the central column will have an impact on the whole energetic form, through every opening through the axis. Most importantly, this model, which is a model, like a word, used to describe the ineffable, suggests that resources from the unified pool of emptiness – demons and angels both – can be allowed into the energetic form and processed, healed or manifested there.

This has implications for psychic development, the healing arts and the deeper realizations connected to our collective responsibility for the whole.

If fear arises, it is important to allow for the possibility that the finest, most enduring aspects of emptiness appear to manifest as in the first instance the Stillness of Silence, the Stillness of Being and the Stillness of Eternity, and behind that as seemingly objective layers of presence indivisibly identifiable as layers of Peace, Love and Unity.

6

The Art of Living

"Turn within. Keep moving until you find a space where you can manifest peace, love and unity. Be that. Live it."

I am here.

It is a statement when said with feeling and physical presence that calls in the disparate parts of us to duty. I am here to be of service.

It is a statement of responsibility. When I am here, I am responsive. When I am here, you are here too. We are here, and something new can be born out of the freedom around that synergy. I am here for you.

Yet, "I am here" is an ongoing creative process of existential manifestation through time and space. The division of pure existential perception seems to be ingeniously designed to the evolutionary need of the human being as existence manifests through matter.

Through the purified windows of consciousness, awareness and emptiness, we have a unique opportunity to manifest the interaction of three universal dimensions – that of peace, love and unity. As such, every moment of human life is precious, bringing individually unique information and evolution to the whole.

To move into and behind these windows of perception is to deepen our intimacy with who we essentially are and our purpose on the planet. As such, we also bring down the walls that separate ourselves and others. As we move into increasing unity of all we perceive and experience, the distinction between inside and outside is diminished.

In terms of practical living, each such process leads to a

deepened ability to manifest who we are and what is needed in this limited lifetime.

We can attain states of stillness through the cultivation of consciousness, awareness and emptiness, yet our ability to stay there will be limited without a refinement of consciousness, awareness and emptiness in trilogy.

The art of living is in creating pathways and bridges between the outer manifestations of our life and these states of stillness, the inner universal resources. When we clear these paths, create these bridges or open channels, we become a living service to existence.

You can access the stillness of silence and experience the bliss of freedom from compulsive thoughts. Yet you still have a mind and personality and transient ego, and will still structure your thoughts, communication and direction through that mind, not least in order to preserve physical life for as long as possible. We are collectively using our minds to uncover the objective scientific and mathematical wonder of creation. We use our minds to compose music, theatre and to create experiences of unity and joy. We use our minds to solve individual and collective problems, such as how to save lives and support physical, psychological and spiritual healing after mass disaster. Should these beautiful minds stay forever still?

It is important not to again get caught in the 'either-or' excuse created by the habitual patterns of mind. It is possible to be in stillness or bliss, and at the same time to dance outwards, surrendering to experience, manifestation, or to whatever phenomena arises. For example we can 'become' a feeling or emotion in its entirety, completely surrendering to it, and the way back to pure existence will emerge in and of itself.

The more we develop our freedom of perception, the more we trust our path inside-out and outside-in. Our empire of living expands, as fear is reduced and we actively become part of the whole on all levels.

In the integrative dance between purer positions of perception and momentary entanglement and absorption in experience, we develop a mastery in which the way is cleared to the depths of who you are, each one equal, each one unique.

You will become increasingly able to centre yourself and to release the less essential imprints of fear, ego or immediate gratification. Your capacity to be present with pain is increased – which in itself is a tremendous service to others.

This is a process of empowerment, freedom and responsibility, leading to the purification of perception of life and beauty. It is an integrated, grounded lifetime journey, one made in unity with humanity. It is also a process which moment by moment brings its own rewards.

This process is happening right now, and every moment you choose to release the hooks that enchain you or another in a given position, to sense what is happening inside and to recognize that we are that which is within this experience, much more than the experience itself.

This perceptive light of life is available to us in every moment of free choice.

I am here for you.

Here Am I – Take Me
Here
Between end and becoming,
an assembly of blood bone and flesh
indifferent as dust,
alive mostly in spaces behind
rib cage shield of love
and lungs doing alchemy
with degrees of illusion
tender muscle and strictest bone
longing to belong

as each particle soaring mindless space
surrenders infinite night
for a bright and empty world.
Am
not all we feared
not the love,
nor terror of children,
forsaken in hollow lands;
nor the great soul spreading
peace in mortal frame,
but being partly whole,
as observing is observing
through ages
of love and bliss
and the incredible loss.
I
with sacred cynicism of words
whisper now, resting helpless
on wings of softness
melting mind surrendered
as wisdom rises no measure
but to affirm it attends.
And humanity is raising a godly head
from sphere of beloved earth,
lost and breaking open,
in loneliness of seeming apart,
he will say:
"Here am I.
Take me. "

Glossary of Terms

Active
The 'active' is used in terms of the pushing, offering or expression of form.

Awakening
A term used for the awakening of consciousness in the centre of the head independently of thoughts, beliefs and stimuli.

Awareness
Perception through feeling, before and beyond language.

Being
The state of pure awareness, undetermined by mental identity, or cognitive time.

Bliss
Refined pleasure or excitement through the intensification of consciousness in physical form.

Cognition
The art of processing data into relative knowledge.

Compassion
The recognition of togetherness in suffering and the passion to be of service – a quality of the dimension of awareness.

Consciousness
The field of perception connected with the head/brain, language, thought and cognition. Existing independently of all the former.

Creation
Life on planet earth as it manifests now, through vibrational initiation.

Ecstasy
The experience of intense happiness arising from the refinement of awareness.

Ego
An artificial sense of self which has been invested with absolute reality. Moves through division and separation.

Empathy
The unconditional experience of suffering free of agenda. A quality of perception through emptiness.

Emptiness
Ubiquitous, space beyond and behind the illusion of an inherently separate self or material form. The intransient.

Emotion
Feeling reactions related to survival, including anger and fear.

Enlightenment
Opening to universal love through the refinement of awareness.

Essential Being
The evolving storehouse of individual qualities.

Existence
Who we are, unconditional to form, yet expressing through and within all form and experience.

Feeling
The sentient aspect of experience, perceived through awareness.

Human
Our highest objective and purpose right now.

Knowledge
The non-absolute sum of all that can be known.

Liberation
Release from the illusion of separation and the freedom to form illusions of choice.

Life
Existence manifesting in form.

Love
A universal and endless source of well-being and nurture, unconditional to processes of creation and destruction. An aspect of existence revealed through the perceptive window of awareness.

Manifestation
Existence through the world of form on all layers and through all aspects.

Meditation
Perceptive travel through the layers of existence.

Non-being
An aspect of the imperceptible, unrevealable and unknowable; connected with the preservation of form and deep sleep.

Observer
The originating presence of unconditioned awareness perceiving through awareness.

Passion
The allowance of suffering as service to the whole.

Peace
The unconditional, universal aspect of existence which is a backdrop to creation.

Pure Being
The state of unconditional awareness, behind, before and coexisting within all manifestation.

Realization
The process of liberation that involves seeing through illusion and the release of beliefs through perception through emptiness.

Receptive
The pulling aspect of form; the invitation or the arousal of form.

Sentience
The ability to feel, perceive, or to experience subjectivity.

Stillness
Non-dual, intransient spaces beyond polarity unconditional to the push, pull, active or receptive forces. Individual, existential dimensions of perspective.

Transformation
The liberation and reformation of form, experience, states.

Time

Patterns of cause and effect; occurrence; the identification of events according to the man-made clock.

Universal

All that is – also that which is beyond human perception – in all dimensions of existence. Includes the possibility of dimensions of non-existence.

Wisdom

The deeper layers of knowledge as arising from the movement of awareness into consciousness and as formed by the mind.

Witness

A satellite of universal consciousness.

About the Author

Georgi (Georgina Yael Johnson) began studying meditation and inner growth when she was 13. With a degree in English Language and Literature from Oxford University, she broadened this spiritual inquiry into an exploration of words and meaning; and the language of the unconscious through an application of psychoanalytic and feminist literary theory.

Georgi is a teacher of the seven year Healing Principle education developed by the international Dutch spiritual teacher and author Bart ten Berge, on the basis of the work of the late Robert Moore. She lives in Israel with her seven children, where she has a private mentoring practice. She is available to give workshops and lectures worldwide to students of inner growth and healing.

BOOKS

O is a symbol of the world, of oneness and unity. In different cultures it also means the "eye," symbolizing knowledge and insight. We aim to publish books that are accessible, constructive and that challenge accepted opinion, both that of academia and the "moral majority."

Our books are available in all good English language bookstores worldwide. If you don't see the book on the shelves ask the bookstore to order it for you, quoting the ISBN number and title. Alternatively you can order online (all major online retail sites carry our titles) or contact the distributor in the relevant country, listed on the copyright page.

See our website **www.o-books.net** for a full list of over 500 titles, growing by 100 a year.

And tune in to myspiritradio.com for our book review radio show, hosted by June-Elleni Laine, where you can listen to the authors discussing their books.

mySpiritRadio